BEST PLACES TO GOLF NORTHWEST

BEST PLACES TO GOLF **NORTHWEST**

BRITISH COLUMBIA TO NORTHERN UTAH,
THE WESTERN ROCKIES TO THE PACIFIC

JEFF WALLACH

SASQUATCH BOOKS
SEATTLE

Again, for R^2

Printed in Singapore by Star Standard Industries Pte Ltd.
Published by Sasquatch Books
Distributed by Publishers Group West
12 11 10 09 08 07 06 05 04   6 5 4 3 2 1

Front cover: Nicklaus North Golf Course: Whistler, British Columbia
Cover photograph: ©John and Jeannine Henebry

Back cover photos (top to bottom) courtesy: Sandpines Golf Links, Port Ludlow Golf Course, Cordova Bay Golf Course, Fairwinds Golf and Country Club, John Douthwaite

Cover design: Stewart A. Williams
Interior design: Kate Basart
Production editor: Cassandra Mitchell

Sasquatch Books
119 South Main Street, Suite 400
Seattle, WA 98104
(206) 467-4300
www.sasquatchbooks.com
custserv@sasquatchbooks.com

Contents

Acknowledgments

Many thanks to all the public relations warriors, marketing magicians, Visitors and Conventions Bureau demigods, patient golf professionals, chefs, restaurant servers and bartenders, resort and hotel staff members, editors of extreme merit, and others who have eased the burden of travel and made writing about golf possibly the best job in America. And, of course, the mojo portion of thanks to my wife, Reneé, who always encouraged me to go.

Introduction

You're holding in your hands a different kind of golf book. It's not a compendium of such lifeless statistics as yardages and slope ratings for every golf course in the Northwest, though some of that information is included. It doesn't cover every last good course in this vast, rugged territory, and you may notice the absence of a favorite layout or two of your own. Prices (because they change so frequently) and par (which is always 70, 71, or 72, and as far as I can tell has never convinced anyone to play or not play a particular golf course) are not listed.

Sure, some of the basics are here, such as what the best season

is and whether a course is a reasonably priced muni, an upscale public venue, or a tony, special-occasion, resort-type layout. In fact, if you want a thumbnail sketch of a particular course or resort, turn to the end of each chapter. Use the lists of phone numbers, websites, and other information to plan a visit to one of these great Northwest golf destinations; read the chapters to be inspired to visit them—and to be entertained. My goal in compiling this book was to breathe some life into golf travel writing—to re-create what it feels like to play these great venues: to face daunting carries over ravines, to execute cut shots over rivers and lakes, to look toward the green down a hallway of Douglas firs or ponderosa pines and see volcanic peaks crowding like an expectant gallery beyond the flag. These stories, I hope, taste like an ocean breeze and give off the rich, coffee-like aroma of a divot freshly unzipped from a thick fairway.

Best Places to Golf: Northwest is about the best golf destinations from British Columbia to northern Utah and between the Pacific Ocean and the Rocky Mountains—destinations worth spending some time in, not only for the obvious attractions that the best northwestern cities and topographies have to offer but also because you could play a different great golf course (or two) in most of these places every day. In addition to so-called golf destinations, the book also presents stand-alone resorts that have high-caliber golf courses, making them destinations in their own right.

Because I not only golf in the Northwest, but also live here, many of these chapters also provide a little local color—about a nearby museum or hike, for example—or offer an occasional restaurant or hotel recommendation. They also introduce a few of the characters I've encountered on Northwest golf courses. Mostly, though, they're about playing golf in places where there's a lot of good golf to be played. Like golf, they're meant to be fun. Consult this book to help

Swan-e-set: Pitt Meadows, British Columbia ▶

plan a vacation to one of these great destinations, or curl up with it during the rainy season when you're daydreaming in your favorite chair about a road trip.

These pages are filled with what I'd tell you on the phone if you called and said you were thinking about playing some golf in Spokane or Sunriver or Salt Lake and wanted my advice. (But please, don't call—I've already told you everything I know.) I hope you enjoy reading these stories even half as much as I enjoyed researching and writing them.

—Jeff Wallach
PORTLAND, OREGON

A note on the information in this book:

Every effort was made to include the best northwestern golf courses clustered together in destinations, or that stand on their own but enjoy affiliation with a resort. All were open to the public at the time of publication. All service information was checked with the management and staffs of the golf courses. However, owners and management shift, prices rise, public courses turn private, and other changes occur. It's always worth phoning ahead to check on rates and availability.

Prices listed for greens fees represent the lowest low-season rate and the highest high-season rate for unrestricted eighteen-hole play. In some cases, cart costs are additional and taxes may also apply. The following system is utilized in this book to represent the range of greens fees:

$ = $25 or less
$$ = $26–$50
$$$ = $51–$75
$$$$ = $76–$100
$$$$$ = more than $100

THE OREGON COAST

WHEN NEW GOLF COURSES like the two layouts at **BANDON DUNES GOLF RESORT** come along—as they do every hundred years or so—it's difficult to describe them because folks have already exhausted all the superlatives in characterizing other, far lesser golf courses. Such layouts form an entirely new vocabulary. The Bandon Dunes Resort is that rare locale that induces a sweet and delicious nostalgia and somehow returns us to ourselves. Just seeing these two collaborations of nature and design makes you want to wave your arms and run wildly down the fairways, yodeling nonsense syllables into the sea air.

Designed with four sets of tees by Scottish architect David Kidd, the original **BANDON DUNES** course

◀ *Bandon Dunes: Bandon, Oregon*

1

plays from 5,125 to 6,732 yards over 250 acres of the most gruffly enchanting and achingly graceful golf terrain this side of Dornoch. Seven holes caper along cliffs overlooking the ocean, but every single hole offers an aspect of crashing surf. The fairways themselves heave and roll like grassed ocean swells, and they're adorned with bunkering so sublime you could weep just looking at their deep shapes and rich, dark colors. The rough, which has been cut low to sedate its potentially punitive remonstrance, contains just enough gorse and Scotch broom to confuse your geography. It could be allowed to turn brutal for tournament play. The greens are huge (number seventeen runs to 17,000 square feet) and curvaceous as a belly dancer, firm yet eminently fair, and designed to 1880s specifications. Simple boardwalks wind through waste areas and around some of the tees, lending a natural, beachy feel.

The course begins boldly and never shrinks into complacency. Number one plays 396 yards from the white tees; whack your drive into a receptive tureen of fescue and Bentgrass, but prepare for a possible blind uphill approach shot that's equal parts faith and hopefulness, over a sandy wasteland edged in beach grass that camouflages the huge, sloping green. Facing this shot is like quaffing a triple espresso, but after the sudden spike in your blood pressure, Bandon Dunes will reassure you with fair, challenging shot-making requests and will dazzle you with its pure elegance. Playing here is like watching a Shakespeare play staged in two acts, each containing nine gripping scenes.

The third hole, a par 5 of 518 yards, calls for a muscular 185-yard carry off the tee. From there, you can look down upon the rest of the layout spread like a green silk flag rippling toward the sea in a salt breeze. Standing with club in hand, you'll feel like Moses in Foot Joys. Number five presents the most memorable hole on the front side; it spills across 423 yards of cliff top overlooking the beach. Your drive must avoid clumps of beach grass dividing the fairway into two slots—one portly and welcoming as Falstaff, the other narrow and bitter as a shrew, perched upon the rim of the abyss but offering a shorter route to the hole. Your second shot must follow a tight gizzard of fairway. Some players will be wise to lay up even though it's a par 4. On the eighth hole, steeply faced bunkers form a barrier 200 yards from the tee of this 351-yarder; they're not too difficult to carry but may prove malignant if you go in. The ninth hole features a cluster of semisunken fairway bunkers dividing the first landing area of a 554-yard odyssey.

The back side begins with a risk/reward option: Play left for a longer shot to a visible pin or hit right over steep bunkers for a shorter but blind approach. Windblown pines frame the ocean view

beyond the green. Thirteen, a par 5 that looks inland toward Oregon's coastal mountains, presents a fairway that ululates for 539 yards like an abstract expressionist painting of green form. Many players will call sixteen the most dramatic on the course, a seaside holiday of 313 yards with a ravine slashing up into the fairway from the beach. It may well provide the best view of any golf hole in North America. Seventeen runs beside a brushy creek and bear-filled ravine that you must negotiate to hit at a misanthropically placed pin. When shadows fall across the linksland, you'll be willing to mortgage your heart for that fleeting pleasure to last. Let's just say that you'll crave haggis and play the bagpipes when you come in from a bracing walk around the true Scottish-style terrain. Walking the course isn't just encouraged but actually required; only medically disabled golfers are allowed to take carts.

If the original course at Bandon causes you to keen like Mel Gibson in *Braveheart*, wait until you play **PACIFIC DUNES**, the second course built at the resort. Architect and cult figure Tom Doak created a 6,623-yard, Irish-accented venue among huge sand blowouts, with another seven holes that stretch languidly along the ocean. Highlights of Pacific Dunes include number four, the first seaside hole; back-to-back par 3s at holes ten and eleven; and an eighteenth that can cause 660 yards of pure, sandy mayhem. Words cannot do justice to this course, which in its first years of existence has broken into the top ten of just about every best-course list compiled.

Walking Pacific, I found myself grinning and shaking my head all day like a guy who'd just discovered a gym bag full of magic lamps washed up on the empty beach. Like old songs, certain holes loosed warm, goosey memories from my youth, not to mention associations with holes at such places as Turnberry, Ballybunion, and the Old and New Courses at St. Andrews. Need I say more?

Bandon Dunes is a four- to five-hour drive from Portland, much of it scenic, all of it fraught with giddy anticipation. The town of Bandon is a sleepy fishing village brimming with character. The resort itself offers lodging in a variety of lodge rooms and cottages and boasts such places to pass time as the Bunker Cigar Bar and a British-style pub, in addition to a fine bar and dining room in the main lodge.

Many golfers en route to Bandon Dunes from Portland and points north stop over at SANDPINES GOLF LINKS in Florence. In 1993, this seaside town put a few zillion acres of dunes to good use by hiring Rees Jones to design these 7,252-yard links, which feature five sets of tees and three signature holes.

The course really begins on the 398-yard fourth hole, replete with trees and hidden bunkers and a green guarded by a lake right and a bunker left. After sweeping through stands of windblown pines, Sandpines provides a knuckle-biting finish as holes sixteen through eighteen bank around a huge lake. The 501-yard finishing hole allows you to gulp as much water as you like as you try (if you're playing from shorter tees) to reach the well-protected green in two.

Heading farther north up the coast, you'll encounter one of Oregon's original golf resort destinations: **SALISHAN LODGE**. The two men the starter paired me up with on the first tee of the **SALISHAN GOLF LINKS** had stopped in for a quick eighteen between bouts of salmon fishing in a nearby coastal river. They were wearing muddy jeans and checked flannel shirts, which seemed to shout, "This is Oregon!" Yet while Salishan's golf course is a rugged, woodsy affair with a whiskey-rough Scottish accent, the lodge itself is just the place to recivilize you. This combination of earthy outdoors and warm interiors is quintessentially Oregonian.

Although it looks like a worn condo complex from the outside, that's part of Salishan's quiet, understated beauty. Located on a sandy spit between Siletz Bay and the Pacific and surrounded by fragrant forests of red cedar, fir, pine, and spruce, Salishan Lodge was built of local wood to blend with the natural setting. Fireplaces in every guest room perfume the sea air with wood smoke, and views of either the bay, forest, or golf course make this the perfect place to hole up after you've played eighteen (or thirty-six) holes. Covered walkways link even the most secluded rooms to the art gallery, library, wine cellar, fitness center, lounge, and eateries.

Make certain to treat yourself to dinner in the Dining Room, which boasts a menu combining traditional fare with Northwestern flare. As always happens when I travel with my wife, her menu choices seemed far better than my own: I coveted her alder-plank salmon with pinot noir shallot jus—perhaps the tastiest fish I've ever had to surreptitiously attack. I also pined for her Vienna basket dessert—a crispy pastry shell drizzled with chocolate and filled with light cream and berries; she had to fend me off with her fork. All meals at Salishan can be accompanied by the perfect wine because the renowned cellar houses more than eight thousand bottles.

The name "Salishan" is derived from the Northwest's Salish Indians and means "a coming together from diverse points to communicate in harmony." This aptly describes how you might approach the greens on some of Salishan's golf holes—from points as diverse as uphill and downhill lies, deep forest, beach grasses, dunes, and thick

8

rough. Only the "harmony" part may seem misleading, unless you make par.

In playing the course, heed this wisdom borrowed from Royal Troon and once displayed on a plaque above the pro shop door: "As much by skill as by strength." The course, originally designed by Fred Federspiel, was renovated by Bill Robinson. The project included extending water hazards and adding much needed irrigation, a few bunkers to force long hitters to also be more precise, and all sorts of lovely berms and mounding to delineate fairways and better separate the holes and to increase the Scottish links feel. At the time of this writing, PGA touring pro, golf architect, and local funny-man Peter Jacobsen was slated to further spruce up the course.

Salishan Golf Links really consists of two very distinct nines. The front weaves through thick, forested hillsides with small, speedy greens guarded by traps as overprotective as my own mother. The back, known as the "ocean nine," offers views of crashing waves, and its fairways are framed by sand dunes and beach grasses. Wind is also a major factor; if you're not careful, you're likely to see your clubs flying toward the pin in a big gust. Consider placing stones in the pockets of skinny playing partners. To make things just a little more difficult, quite a few holes on the course dogleg left, which might help lefties and force righty slicers to work that much harder.

Number twelve is possibly the most ornery hole on the course—a 433-yard par 4 that plays along a narrow, dune-lined fairway to a small green embraced by deep traps and unforgiving rough. Two trees guard the corner of the fairway where the hole turns slightly to the right; you'll hear the ocean pounding just beyond the green. Throughout the course beware of an edible plant, salal, that lines some fairways—it's as bitter to hit out of as it is on the tongue.

Potentially easy holes (if you hit the right shots) include the tenth—a short par 5 (446 yards) that's reachable with a drive and a long iron if you stay out of encroaching water on the tee shot—and number seventeen, a par 4 that you might reach from the tee with a steady wind and several months of clean living behind you, although bunkers lurk in dangerous locations here. Salishan's greens are lightning fast: On a dry day, bring a radar gun for an accurate reading. While the course doesn't seem overly difficult, only a handful of players have broken 70 here in nearly forty years of play.

You must play Salishan several times to appreciate how the course changes with wind, weather, and light. Noticing such subtleties may also provide a key to understanding the quirky, individualistic local character that leads Oregonians to play golf twelve months of the

11

year even though it rains through six of them. On days when coastal weather sweeps across the weathered coast, pull out your Gore-Tex and simply hit an extra club or two. A blazing fire awaits back in your lodge room, where you can blame any bad shots on the misanthropic but freshening wind.

Ninety scenic minutes northwest of Portland, and a short jaunt farther up the coast from Salishan, lies the refreshingly unknown **GEARHART GOLF LINKS AND RESORT**. The second-oldest course in the West, Gearhart opened in 1892 with four holes. Over the years, a number of designers—including the renowned H. Chandler Egan—left their mark on the layout. In 1999 the links received a full makeover in the talented hands of William Robinson, who replaced all tees and bunkers as well as several greens, installed new irrigation, and otherwise pepped things up. The new 21,000 square-foot Victorian clubhouse recalls the original 1900s-era hotel. Lodging is available across the street from the clubhouse at the Gearhart by the Sea condominiums.

Gearhart is a true links course that rolls and dips among moundy, grass-covered dunes. The ocean only provides subtext here, remaining just out of sight, although you can hear and feel it. The 6,218-yard layout is charming and subtle. The front side careens along nicely, if uneventfully, until the fine number five, a 372-yard dogleg left with a narrow landing area. Even a slightly mishit drive may leave a difficult approach over a pond to a small green. Number ten, at 341 yards, also excels, with angled bunkers creating a landing area that widens further from the tee, an enticement to long hitters. Throughout the course, narrow ridges and other topographical features carom balls every which way, so consider where you want them to end up. Gearhart provides a breezy adventure in classic links golf.

The sleepy town of Gearhart is perfect for beach walks and gallery browsing, the kind of place Portlanders have retreated to for over a century—these days to rent weathered Cape Cod–style beach houses where they cook fresh local seafood and read. Elsewhere along this part of the scenic coast—tucked between crashing surf and Pacific forests—you can tour the cheese factory or glide through the Air Museum in Tillamook, visit lighthouses and Lewis-and-Clark historic sites, fish, kayak, hike the headlands of a number of state parks, or visit kitschy shops and chowder houses before retreating to a bed and breakfast or a room right at the resort. The north coast's attractions are quiet and understated. Down U.S. 101 in Seaside and Canon Beach, the action—in the form of skee ball arcades, a good bookstore, and a long promenade from the turn of the century—climbs a notch.

BANDON DUNES GOLF RESORT

57744 Round Lake Drive, Bandon, OR 97411
888-345-6008 • www.bandondunesgolf.com

Bandon Dunes

Architect/Year: David Kidd, 1999
Tees/Yardages: 4 sets of tees from 5,125 to 6,732 yards
Season: Year-round
Cost: $$$ to $$$$$, replay $$ to $$$$
Tee times: Resort guests no restrictions, nonguests up to 3 weeks in advance

Pacific Dunes

Architect/Year: Tom Doak, 2001
Tees/Yardages: 4 sets of tees from 5,107 to 6,623 yards
Season: Year-round
Cost: $$$-$$$$$, replay $$ to $$$$
Tee times: Resort guests no restrictions, nonguests up to 3 weeks in advance

GEARHART GOLF LINKS AND RESORT

1157 N Marion Street, Gearhart, OR 97138
503-717-9243 • www.gearhartgolflinks.com
Architects/Years: Unknown, 1892; renovated by William Robinson, 1999
Tees/Yardages: 3 sets of tees from 5,353 to 6,218 yards
Season: Year-round
Cost: $$
Tee times: Up to 2 weeks in advance

SALISHAN LODGE

7760 Highway 101 N, Gleneden Beach, OR 97388
800-890-0387 • www.salishan.com
Architect/Year: Fred Federspiel, 1965
Tees/Yardages: 3 sets of tees from 5,331 to 6,453 yards
Season: Year-round
Cost: $$ to $$$
Tee times: Resort guests no restrictions, nonguests up to 2 weeks in advance

SANDPINES GOLF LINKS

1201 35th Street, Florence, OR 97439
800-917-4653 • www.sandpines.com
Architect/Year: Rees Jones, 1993
Tees/Yardages: 5 sets of tees from 5,346 to 7,252 yards
Season: Year-round
Cost: $$ to $$$
Tee times: Up to 2 months in advance

PORTLAND AND ENVIRONS

IF I WERE SMART, I wouldn't tell you anything about my hometown of Portland, Oregon. I would not mention that this green, eclectic, and eminently habitable hamlet of half a million lucky people (1.9 million including the surrounding area) located equally near to an ocean and a glacier has been ranked by such magazines as *Money* and *Travel & Leisure* as among the most livable cities in America. I wouldn't even whisper that parks and fountains are as ubiquitous as the coffee shops and handcrafted beers Portland is known for. In fact, Portland is home to both the smallest park (24-inch Mill's End) and the largest urban wilderness (5,000-acre Forest Park) in the United States. It also contains a city park built on a dormant volcano (Mount Tabor).

◀ *Stone Creek: Oregon City, Oregon*

17

As for the handcrafted beers, the local McMenamin brothers are famous for their string of microbreweries in combination with vintage movie theaters (The Mission Theater, The Bagdad Theater), concert venues (The Crystal Ballroom), and unique hotels (among others, The Kennedy School, where the guest rooms are converted grade school classrooms and the Detention Room is a cigar bar). The Bridgeport Brewery offers two Portland pubs—the Northwest neighborhood's brick brewery and the Hawthorne Street edition with great food and livelier action. The Lucky Labrador Brewpub welcomes dogs to the outside seating area and pours a great stout.

Portland's many and varied neighborhoods include the artsy Pearl, trendy Nob Hill, antique row in Sellwood, and the Hawthorne district, which the *London Times* described as "a beguiling mixture of gentrification and radicalism." The city's distinctive sectors repose on both sides of the Willamette River, which is crossed by nearly a dozen bridges. Mass transit rules here, with light rail, cable cars, and other forms of modern people movers. People are moved, too, by the natural beauty of the surrounding snowcapped peaks, verdant valleys, abundant waterfalls, and accessible high desert. They're moved to shop by the fact that Oregon has no sales tax. Portland also boasts several world-class museums, performing arts centers, and gaggles

Langdon Farms: Aurora, Oregon
▶

of galleries and public sculpture, murals, and other forms of creative expression. For what it's worth, the city also lays claim to the song "Louie Louie," which was supposedly written there, though nobody claims to understand a word of it. Portland's Rose Garden Arena is home to the basketball-playing Trailblazers, who have been breaking the hearts of local fans (partly by spending as much time in criminal court as on the basketball court) since Bill Walton left town.

By now you're probably hungry, so it's time to enjoy the fresh, creative regional cuisine (in James Beard's hometown) at such eateries as Higgins and Wildwood. You'll find a wealth of great hotels, too, ranging from the Old World elegance of the Heathman to the boutiquey new Paramount to the Avalon Hotel and Spa, set on a greenbelt overlooking the river.

This hip, high-tech, sandal-wearing city also offers enough top-drawer urban golf venues to keep you busy until the cows come home. In the early part of the twentieth century, Portland boasted more golf holes per capita than any other city in the United States. (Currently, it seems to boast the most double lattes and body piercings.) Golf around Portland is still accessible, inexpensive, and excellent, especially since a construction boom during the 1990s brought a handful of great modern courses online. Golf orgiasts can mix a cocktail of old classic designs with spanky new venues, easily play thirty-six holes a day in the late light of summer, and then relax in—or outside of—a lovely, quirky city bustling with everything that makes a place strike just the right chord in your heart.

Portland's golf courses are always lush and green from the ample rainfall, but summer weather is reliably sunny and warm. Autumn delivers crisp days, changing leaves, and often plenty of sunshine through October. In winter and early spring, locals slog around the fairways in knee-high clamming boots fit with golf spikes. Bring plenty of Gore-Tex outerwear if you visit between November and May.

You needn't venture far from downtown to enjoy some of Portland's finest golf. For that matter, you barely need to leave the airport. Convenient to the city core and close enough to PDX's runways to hear an airline safety talk, the two Robert Trent Jones Jr. layouts at **HERON LAKES GOLF COURSE** dance lightly through wetlands just north of town. The courses comprise the best thirty-six holes of the Portland 90, a series of munis owned by the city. Heron Lakes's **GREENBACK** course (named after a duck) tops out at 6,608 yards and purveys a traditional design punctuated by elevated greens, occasional forced carries over water, and bold, strategic calls. One local pro describes the 207-yard par-3 sixteenth as "one of the hardest on

the planet" because it requires a perfect two-iron when the wind is ripping in your face. The Greenback Course recalls Jones's father's work—a tidy classic venue in the old style.

But Jones Jr.'s **GREAT BLUE** (as in heron) is the bird of paradise here. The 6,902-yard track's open fairways ramble between Scottish-style mounds and pose a collection of excellent risk/reward riddles while offering views of 11,245-foot Mount Hood. Many locals consider the 466-yard par-4 eighth hole among the toughest to solve. Big hitters can attempt to squeak a long drive between a line of trees and a slough that guard the left-doglegging fairway, but registered conservatives will opt for a three-wood aimed at a directional bunker, leaving a *long* shot into the tucked green. Great Blue's three finishing holes all present the classic backpacker's dilemma: how much water to carry. The sixteenth fairway is actually split by a lake and by wetlands; only monsters and lunatics will try to thread a shot between these for an easier approach, although during the annual Quarterback Shootout held here, one former professional ball tosser made a hole-in-one double eagle. Great Blue doesn't contain a single uneventful hole, and a number of quirky greens tucked behind ponds provide ample opportunities for heroism or sheepishness.

Portlanders have been enjoying classic golf at **EASTMORELAND GOLF**

◀ *Pumpkin Ridge:*
North Plains, Oregon

COURSE since H. Chandler Egan designed the 6,529-yard layout on the eastern outskirts of town in 1918. Eastmoreland romps through lowlands surrounded by natural springs, rhododendron gardens, and galleries of yapping ducks and excited waterfowl. It's also a veritable arboretum of huge old trees. Eastmoreland is one of those courses that looks easy yet still manages to beat the stuffing out of you with uneven lies, crowned or subtly sloped greens, and plenty of shrubbery to trim with mishit shots. The course opens gently with a 310-yard par 4 with a devious putting surface. Walter Hagen once said that the 462-yard thirteenth, a par 5 with a ravine and huge green-fronting swale, was one of the best holes he'd ever played. The seventeenth, a 150-yard poke to a peninsula green, is the determining factor in many matches.

Forty minutes west of Portland toward the Coast Range, Bob Cupp's **PUMPKIN RIDGE GOLF CLUB** spooks some golfers with its bag full of tricks and treats. Pumpkin was the site of the 1997 and 2003 U.S. Women's Opens, the location of Tiger's third U.S. Amateur win in 1996, and host to Nike Tour events and other tournaments. It was also Oregon's first upscale public/private golf complex when it opened in the early 1990s. The public-side **GHOST CREEK** course explains why Charlie Brown's friend Linus sat out in a field with his golf clubs waiting for The Great Pumpkin, and this is as great as a pumpkin gets. *GOLF Magazine* ranks Ghost Creek among the top one hundred courses in the United States.

The 6,839-yard par-71 Bentgrass track exudes a rugged, clean-cut feel as it whisks through forests of fir, maple, ash, and oak, meanders through open meadows, and curls around two lakes. Cupp endowed the layout with classical bunkers featuring overhanging edges, which create dark, shadowy places where goblins may gobble golf balls. The frolicking creek after which the course is named disappears and reappears without warning like an elusive specter. Watch for it on number six, for example, a 371-yard slant left where the creek begins right about where the fairway bunkers do, tightening the landing area. Watch out for the triple-bogeyman, too. The ninth hole, a mere 469 yards of par 4, features a large lake and two streams. Number eighteen provides a 454-yard opportunity to ghostbust by reaching the well-protected green in two without splashing. Who ya gonna call when you run out of golf balls?

A short drive from Pumpkin Ridge, **THE RESERVE VINEYARDS AND GOLF CLUB** decants two thirst-quenching wine-themed courses, North and South, designed by Bob Cupp and John Fought, respectively. The facility rotates the two tracks between public and private play twice a month—something that's great for the game. The entire complex is decorated with grapevine icons and even has its own wine label.

You may produce a few whines of your own if you misplace your "A" game—although the Fought and Cupp courses are more likely to elicit Bacchanalian delight. The Cupp Course, now called the **NORTH COURSE**, runneth over with 6,845 yards of heathland-style golf featuring such modern elements as rolling mounds and distinctive ground shaping, short-grass green surrounds, tough putting surfaces, and what may well be the only triple green in the world. Put on your thinking cap for holes such as number seven, 289 yards from the blue tees with a tree guarding the green; you'll want to leave your woods (and possibly your golf ball) in the bag. Sip from the Cupp's directional bunkers and other lovely subtleties and you'll feel warm all over.

The Fought Course, now known as the **SOUTH COURSE**, pours more like a bold cabernet, though a sandy one, as more than a hundred bunkers (in the tradition of Tillinghast at Winged Foot) speckle this venerable layout that winds through mature trees over natural terrain. If you're like me, you might play the entire layout without landing on grass—although I don't recommend this, as grass is much softer than sand and doesn't get in your eyes. Reaching to 7,172 yards from

The Reserve: Aloha, Oregon ▶

the tips with three par 3s over 200 yards, Fought's layout may leave you feeling like a barrel full of stomped grapes. A rock-walled creek appears in several places, such as on number ten, where it crosses the fairway. Imbibe this delicious vintage Fought layout—with classic overtones, heady bouquet, and a bold, turfy nose—and still wake up without a hangover.

Whoever told me that I couldn't hit the side of a barn with a golf shot should have seen me at **LANGDON FARMS GOLF CLUB**, twenty minutes south of Portland. Designed by Bob Cupp in partnership with

◄ *OGA Member's Course: Woodburn, Oregon*

John Fought, the par-71, 6,931-yard layout expresses a farm theme, with the aforementioned red barn (built in 1918) decorating the eighth hole. The depressed fairway design is actually quite uplifting—lovely containment mounds impart the sense that you're golfing through soft, grassy canyons. Mounds rise alongside the short grass, virtually hugging the landing areas, and kicking some wayward shots back homeward but also making for occasionally enigmatic lies. Langdon's highlights include amusing rooster tee markers, fabulous service, a covered range, church pew bunkers, and a par 3 of 125 yards that may be the toughest hole on the course; it's like chipping onto the top of a bowling ball. Design elements such as colorful wildflowers, stone walls, and bridges add to Langdon's charm.

Amid a pandemic of so-called upscale-daily-fee golf designs (often meaning, simply, "overpriced"), it's refreshing to encounter an admittedly affordable new public venue without pretensions. Designed by Peter Jacobsen and Jim Hardy, **STONE CREEK GOLF CLUB**, thirty minutes southeast of Portland, is a role model of sincere public golf. The architects maximized the potential of an unremarkable site that once housed a turkey farm but still retains plenty of stately firs. Jacobsen says, "We built this golf course economically at a time when the price of golf courses was spiraling up and the cost to play golf was spiraling up. We fired a shot across the decks of all those people and said, 'Look, you can do this economically and be able to play affordable golf.'"

Three lakes reflect the ever-changing Oregon sky at Stone Creek, and distant glances offer views of glacier-capped Mount Hood. Four sets of tees play as long as 6,873 yards. A number of holes are decorated with huge, orange, naturally sculpted boulders that lend the course its name. The welcoming, sweepy greens are immaculate.

Stone Creek's first few holes rollick through open meadowlands before darting into the forest. Number four, a 498-yard par 5, wends between trees and water en route to a green containing a Scottish "toe" where players can bail out rather than straining to carry a sea of bunkers to the heart of the putting surface. From the toe, the meek will inherit an amusingly steep putt up over a ridge. The 151-yard sixth hole was the site of my first (and only, so far) hole in one, scored during my first outing with a local men's club that has not invited me back since I won all their money. The ninth hole also entertains with a split fairway, one half of which tunnels between a canyon of angled bunkers.

Holes twelve through fifteen are Stone Creek's rock-solid heart, featuring tree-lined fairways, forced carries, elevation changes, and several blind shots. Number fourteen, at 141 yards, calls for a surgical strike over wetlands to a sort of putting patio held up by the ubiquitous giant boulders.

The **OREGON GOLF ASSOCIATION (OGA) MEMBERS COURSE AT TUKWILA** may have one of the longest names around, but it's also long on great golf. Bill Robinson stitched together this tapestry of holes in Woodburn, forty minutes south of Portland. The fabric of Bentgrass stretches 6,650 from the longest of four sets of tees and boasts a couple of reachable (and especially good) par 5s, a huge double green at nine and eighteen, and some of the finest putting surfaces in the region. Water, wicked bunkers, and pesky woods are also on the menu of this stupendous walking course.

The holes here are pure and clever. The OGA course opens with an inviting slight dog right followed by the opposite dog, but this one has more bite— in the form of a hazelnut orchard right, a pond left, and a tree and bunkers that could come into play. Number four is a complex 516 yards: Blind tee shots run down toward a ravine. The second shot climbs back uphill between bunkers and forest and over the chasm to a plateau green. A second par 5 follows. The back side contains the best par 3 on the course, a volatile 172 yards that slope toward water. Fourteen is another strategic 517-yard puzzler that can be solved in several ways, all of which require at least one ravine crossing.

Although the Willamette Valley is the grass seed capital of the world, an even more enticing product grows close to great golf: grapes—as in wine grapes, as in some of the best pinot noirs ever fermented. The most intoxicating nongolf activity in the valley is wine tasting, with a bit of antiquing thrown in. Try a side trip to McMinville, close to the OGA course (and not far from Pumpkin Ridge and the Reserve), where you'll find more than a half-dozen wineries, including the well-loved Eyrie Vineyards, which is open by appointment for tasting wines with complex fruit flavors, aromatic nuances, and sea breezes. Also try Eyrie's product—along with others—at the Oregon Wine Tasting Room nine miles south of McMinville. The driving between sips is pastoral, with views of the Coast Range Mountains, small Old-Western towns, and cute shops. If you'd rather leave the driving to someone else, Grape Escape Winery Tours offers half-day, full-day, and evening outings, most of which stop at three wineries.

Recognizing the symbiotic relationship between golf and drinking, most golf courses offer at least a humble place for a tired hacker to sip a pint after a grueling round. At the McMenamin's Edgefield

*Resort at the Mountain:
Welches, Oregon* ▶

Pub and Brewery twenty minutes east of Portland, managers took the opposite approach: They actually built a golf course for patrons to enjoy with one of the brewery's personable handcrafted beers.

Originally built in 1911 as the Multnomah County Poor Farm, the vast Edgefield property was bought by the entrepreneurial McMenamin brothers, who created a complex of hotel rooms, music venues, restaurants, gardens, theater, winery, and gallery. But the McMenamins were also sharp enough to eventually realize that one essential element was missing: golf.

The 991-yard eighteen-hole **PUB COURSE AT MCMENAMIN'S EDGEFIELD** winds through hills of blackberry bushes overlooking the rest of the unique estate. Holes range from 40 to 80 yards and most require perfect carries to immaculately maintained greens set amid thick, thorny flora. The informal venue (where sixsomes are not unwelcome) features holes named Ruins, Pump House, Flash Flood, and Chute. Perhaps the greatest draw of the Pub Course is that players can stop several times during their round to retrieve a Terminator Stout or Hammerhead Ale from the Distillery Bar or the Red Shed, strategically located along the routing.

An hour east of downtown Portland, the town of Welches—home to the **RESORT AT THE MOUNTAIN**—has been attracting hotel guests since 1893 and golfers since 1928. Nestled at the foot of Mount Hood, the resort has acquired a Scottish accent, discernible in such touches as Scottie-dog tee markers and its very own tartan. Though visitors can hike, fish, raft, ride horses, play tennis and croquet, and even ski nearby in summer, twenty-seven distractions show up in the form of golf holes. The **FOXGLOVE**, **THISTLE**, and **PINE CONE** nines make for a great walk and potentially great scores. Stretching to a maximum length of 6,405 yards, any eighteen-hole combination will provide a handful of challenging holes, several unforgettably beautiful ones, and plenty of others that will simply make you glad to be out beneath old-growth forest in the shadows of the Cascade Mountains. A number of renovations performed in consultation with architect John Harbottle include seven new greens, additional tee boxes, and improved fish passage for threatened salmon and steelhead on the property.

The first hole on the Foxglove nine plays 311 yards over a mid-fairway boulder, and those cutting the dogleg may have a shot at the green or else hear the echo of surlyn on stone. Thistle number one proffers a view of the Hunchback, an El Capitan–like rock face. With its new tee box set on a rock slide back in the woods, 460-yard Pine Cone number five is now a fun, birdie-able par 5 rather than a straightforward (read: boring) par 4.

If you happen to visit Portland on a golf trip—and if you by some chance stop in at any of the courses, bars, restaurants, hotels, galleries, or other attractions that I've referred to here—do me a favor and leave my name out of it. If you asked me, I'd simply tell you that it rains here all the time and the locals are ornery.

EASTMORELAND GOLF COURSE

2425 SE Bybee Boulevard, Portland, OR 97202
503-775-2900
Architect/Year: H. Chandler Egan, 1918
Tees/Yardages: 3 sets of tees from 5,646 to 6,529 yards
Season: Year-round
Cost: $ to $$
Tee times: Up to 1 week in advance in person, up to 6 days in advance by phone

HERON LAKES GOLF COURSE

3500 N Victory Boulevard, Portland, OR 97211
503-289-1818 • www.heronlakesgolf.com

Great Blue

Architect/Year: Robert Trent Jones Jr., 1992
Tees/Yardages: 4 sets of tees from 5,258 to 6,902 yards
Season: Year-round
Cost: $ to $$
Tee times: Up to 1 week in advance in person, up to 6 days in advance by phone/Internet

Greenback

Architect/Year: Robert Trent Jones Jr., 1971
Tees/Yardages: 3 sets of tees from 5,240 to 6,608 yards
Season: Year-round
Cost: $ to $$
Tee times: Up to 1 week in advance in person, up to 6 days in advance by phone/Internet

LANGDON FARMS GOLF CLUB

24377 NE Airport Road, Aurora, OR 97002
503-678-4653 • www.langdonfarms.com

Architects/Year: Bob Cupp and John Fought, 1995
Tees/Yardages: 4 sets of tees from 5,246 to 6,931 yards
Season: Year-round
Cost: $$ to $$$$
Tee times: Up to 30 days in advance

OREGON GOLF ASSOCIATION MEMBERS COURSE AT TUKWILA

2850 Hazelnut Drive, Woodburn, OR 97071
503-981-6105
Architect/Year: Bill Robinson, 1994
Tees/Yardages: 3 sets of tees from 5,498 to 6,650 yards
Season: Year-round
Cost: $$ to $$$
Tee times: Up to 5 days in advance

THE PUB COURSE AT MCMENAMIN'S EDGEFIELD

2126 SW Halsey, Troutdale, OR 97060
800-669-8610 • www.mcmenamins.com
Architect/Year: Darrell Bernhardt, 1998
Tees/Yardages: 1 set of tees, 991 yards
Season: Year-round
Cost: $
Tee times: Up to 6 months in advance

PUMPKIN RIDGE GOLF CLUB

12930 Old Pumpkin Ridge Rd, North Plains, OR 97133
888-594-4653 • www.pumpkinridge.com
Architect/Year: Bob Cupp, 1992
Tees/Yardages: 4 sets of tees from 5,111 to 6,839 yards
Season: Year-round
Cost: $$ to $$$$$
Tee times: Up to 1 week in advance

THE RESERVE VINEYARDS AND GOLF CLUB

4805 SW 229th Avenue, Aloha, OR 97007
503-649-8191 • www.reservegolf.com

North Course

Architect/Year: Bob Cupp, 1998
Tees/Yardages: 4 sets of tees from 5,278 to 6,845 yards
Season: Year-round
Cost: $$ to $$$$
Tee times: Up to 2 weeks in advance

South Course

Architect/Year: John Fought, 1997
Tees/Yardages: 4 sets of tees from 5,189 to 7,172 yards
Season: Year-round
Cost: $$ to $$$$
Tee times: Up to 2 weeks in advance

RESORT AT THE MOUNTAIN

68010 E Fairway Avenue, Welches, OR 97067
800-669-4653 • www.theresort.com

Pine Cone (nine holes)

Architects/Years: Billy Welch, 1928; redesigned Tony
Lasher, 2001
Tees/Yardages: 4 sets of tees from 2,427 to 3,299 yards
Season: Year-round
Cost: $$
Tee times: Resort guests no restrictions, nonguests up
to 2 weeks in advance

Thistle (nine holes)

Architects/Years: Gene Bowman, 1960s; redesigned
Tony Lasher, 2001
Tees/Yardages: 4 sets of tees from 2,238 to 2,956 yards
Season: Year-round
Cost: $$
Tee times: Resort guests no restrictions, nonguests up
to 2 weeks in advance

Foxglove (nine holes)

Architects/Years: Unknown, 1981; redesigned Tony
Lasher, 2001
Tees/Yardages: 4 sets of tees from 2,539 to 3,106 yards
Season: Year-round
Cost: $$
Tee times: Resort guests no restrictions, nonguests up
to 2 weeks in advance

STONE CREEK GOLF CLUB

14603 S Stoneridge Drive, Oregon City, OR 97045
503-518-4653 • www.stonecreekgolfclub.net
Architects/Year: Peter Jacobsen and Jim Hardy, 2002
Tees/Yardages: 4 sets of tees from 5,191 to 6,873 yards
Season: Year-round
Cost: $ to $$
Tee times: Up to 1 week in advance in person, up to 6
days in advance by phone

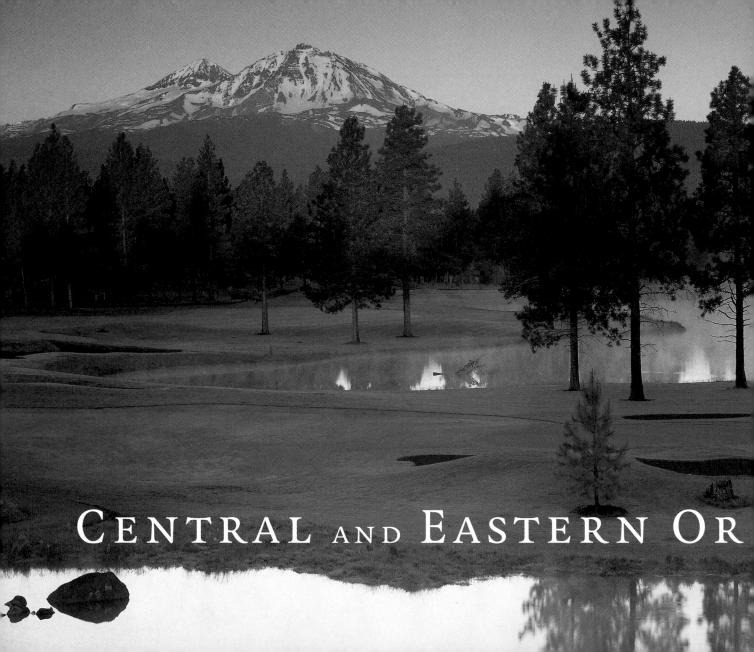

CENTRAL AND EASTERN OR

GON

ONE HUNDRED and eighty miles southeast of Portland lies the high desert town of Bend. The key direction here is east—as in east of the Cascade Mountains, which protect the central part of the state from Pacific storms, providing this town of nearly sixty thousand at an elevation of 3,600 feet with something like 364 days of sunshine annually.

A couple million years back, volcanoes shaped the jagged, snowcapped mountains, clear trout streams, blue lakes, and grasslands that make Central Oregon so spectacular. Native Americans recognized this beauty centuries ago, but Lewis and Clark (among the first Anglo visitors) dismissed the region because it wasn't suitable for farming. More

◀ *Aspen Lakes: Sisters, Oregon*

recently, former governor Neil Goldschmidt described the town of Bend as "in the middle of nowhere," which is exactly the point.

Fueled by the timber industry and the railroads, Bend was the fastest-growing city in the United States between 1910 and 1920. When timber tanked in the seventies and eighties, locals began harvesting tourists instead, who came to hike, climb, fly-fish, bike, ski, and raft. The recreation boom also brought more than two-dozen golf courses that are as lovely and varied as the local wildflowers and which make the Bend area a sort of Palm Springs with a rugged, woodsy, Northwest flare.

During one recent May day in Central Oregon, I downhill skied on Mount Bachelor in the morning, played eighteen holes of golf in the afternoon, took a mountain-bike ride in the evening along the Deschutes River Trail, and considered heading right for the local hospital—but instead went to the Deschutes Brewery for a different sort of medicine. You can do it all in and around Bend, but remember: You don't have to do it all at once.

The Brooks–Scanlon sawmills began operating in Bend in 1915, but by the 1960s, the company realized it would have to diversify to survive. Brooks–Scanlon eventually went into the golf business and created the AWBREY GLEN GOLF CLUB.

Awbrey Glen delivers 7,029 yards of entertaining, delightful, and challenging golf course that couldn't possibly be better maintained. Holes follow the varying terrain the way posses chased outlaws in the Old West—through draws, across "cricks," and in the shadows of buttes and Cascade peaks. En route you'll pass ancient lava flows, twisting juniper trees and pine forests, five blue lakes, grass and sand bunkers, and untold boulders the size of small eastern states. Tees are aimed deceptively and the greens are sloping and fast.

The third hole drops way down into a canyon; if you're attentive, you'll know that sooner or later (on number five) you'll have to hit back up. Number twelve is about as scenic as golf holes get, with cobalt blue lakes and waterfalls glimmering way below the elevated tee. The signature thirteenth hole requires a 157-yard poke through a narrow canyon favored by Native Americans as a power spot. Land on a long green (not Lorne Greene, though he'd feel right at home here) and try to avoid putting over a swale large enough to cover the bodies of several cattle rustlers who failed to make par.

Awbrey Glen is currently a private club, but members of other private clubs can have their pros call to arrange a tee time.

On a glass table in the Great Room inside the **BROKEN TOP CLUB**'s clubhouse, two books caught my attention: *The Native American* and *Golf Resorts of the World*. This juxtaposition defines the spirit of the club and golf course, which combine deep luxury with a close feel for the land and legacy of the region. The clubhouse expresses a Wild West character, mixing raw-beamed construction, leather and Native-patterned couches, cedar, glass, copper, and stone. The club is named for a distinctive volcanic peak visible from the property. The golf course, home to a Seniors Championship event, and the crowning glory of the partnership between designers Tom Weiskopf and Jay Morrish, blends the same expansive outdoorsiness with a sense of peaceful contemplation.

Although a note from your mother won't carry any weight, members of other private clubs located more than 125 miles away can secure a tee time with a note from their local pro. Service is crisp and seamless, and the course itself is often empty.

Weiskopf and Morrish's masterpiece plays 7,165 yards from the backs, but you should get a note from your psychiatrist before taking it on from there. Holes wend through your typical Central Oregon landscape of meadows, forests, swelling hills, and huge rock outcroppings. Although years ago conditions were sometimes sketchy, the course superintendent has been hard at work yelling at the brown patches and encouraging the Bentgrass and Kentucky blue.

From the first tee, Broken Top, is a thinking person's course. The excellent opening hole doglegs left around a couple of bunkers that skew perspective and force you to think about and shape your shots. With a couple of exceptions, the holes are full of personality, at various times perky, entertaining, exhilarating, and downright drop-dead gorgeous—such as number five, a long downhill par 3 with a lake and sand complex to the left and a couple of stately trees standing

Meadows Course:
Sunriver Resort,
Sunriver, Oregon ▶

43

sentry to the right of the green. The course guide claims that the 232-yarder contains enough water and sand for Frankie and Annette to film a beach movie. You may actually be disappointed by the signature eleventh hole. While the approach over a 45-foot vertical pumice wall is unique and dramatic, the blind, unfair green robs the hole of star status.

Located thirty minutes from Bend, in Redmond, **EAGLE CREST RESORT** was one of the first golf destinations built in Central Oregon and presaged the coming boom. The property encompasses two full-size courses—Ridge and Resort—that provide a relaxing respite from some of the region's tougher venues. The **RIDGE COURSE**, the superior layout, is easy and breezy, with views of the Ochoco and Cascade Mountains and a routing through old-growth juniper trees. Designed by John Thronson, Ridge's five tees stretch to 6,927 yards. Greens are faster than the women who once populated nearby saloons—and big. If you feel smug because you hit so many in regulation, check how many times you still need three more strokes to get in the hole. The **RESORT COURSE**, designed by local architect Gene "Bunny" Mason, plays to 6,673 yards. Eagle Crest also offers the shorter **MID-IRONS COURSE** and a beautiful putting course replete with sand traps, juniper trees, wildflowers, and rock gardens. Resort

guests can play golf year-round at Eagle Crest and enjoy 1.5 miles of Deschutes River frontage.

A few miles outside the pretty, Old-Western town of Sisters, **ASPEN LAKES GOLF COURSE**—designed by William Overdorf—currently offers eighteen of the quietest holes you'll ever play. The first Oregon golf course to be enrolled in the Audubon Signature Cooperative Sanctuary Program, Aspen Lakes provides a wild, contemplative 7,302-yard tour through all that's beautiful in the region. Pines, junipers, lakes, native grasses, wildflowers, and bunkers filled with red cinders provide a dramatic counterpoint to green grass and black volcanic peaks in the distance. The current layout includes the **FAITH** and **HOPE** nines. **CHARITY**, the third nine (all are named for peaks of the Three Sisters mountains) will feature water on every hole when it's complete.

Eight miles from Sisters lies **BLACK BUTTE RANCH**, a residential resort community that offers play on two courses: **BIG MEADOW** and **GLAZE MEADOW**. Both layouts on this 1,800-acre property are lined by cheering throngs of ponderosa pines. Big Meadow, designed by Robert Muir Graves, tops out at 6,850 yards. Glaze Meadow, the work of Bunny Mason, stretches to 6,547 yards. Resort guests can choose from a cornucopia of condos and homes to inhabit between golf rounds.

You can't talk about Central Oregon without mentioning the mother of all golf destinations: lovely **SUNRIVER RESORT**. It all began at Sunriver when fur trappers gathered in meadows along the Deschutes River 150 years ago. Now the only traps to worry about were set by course architects throughout the property's fifty-four excellent and varied holes. Located on thirty-three hundred acres fifteen miles south of Bend, the resort lies at the center of one of the most delightful, unpretentious communities you'll never want to leave.

Once a sort of down-home favorite getaway for Oregonians, Sunriver entered the national vocabulary with the word **CROSSWATER**, which for my money is one of the most spectacular designs in America. How about two hundred acres of Bob Cupp–designed target golf where Bentgrass fairways, tees, and greens offset bluegrass and golden fescue; where the routing winds through meadows, among enormous pines and across bird-filled wetlands, while huge volcanic peaks beckon in the distance? If that's not enough, add the clear blue Little Deschutes River for murmuring companionship; holes cross the stream fourteen times, though you won't always cross all of it on the first try. Don't even think about playing Crosswater from its full length of 7,683 yards unless you're suicidal or enjoy the sound of golf balls splashing into hazards. A combination of blue and white tees works best because a few holes lose their character from the whites and may even penalize a long drive hit from those tees. From the back tees, Crosswater is pure carnage. The course may provide the prettiest round you've ever lost a box of Titleists on.

Crosswater opens with calm subtlety—a wide fairway with a handful of defining bunkers—like the beginning of an epic symphony that starts with a few clear, pure tones. The second hole introduces water and a few more trees. The third, a short par 3, offers up a view of Newberry Crater in the background. By the fourth hole, wetlands enter the concert, and the Little Deschutes makes its entry on number five, among the toughest holes on the course. The 460-yard epic par 4 requires a long but precise carry over the river but short of containment bunkers and woods. The long approach demands another wetlands crossing, and the long, narrow green is divided by what seems like a buried tractor trailer. But don't relax even if you somehow manage to make par here because the next hole is 635 yards long.

With all the instruments in place, the tension builds in sweeping and dramatic melodies for the rest of the afternoon—lupines and forced carries, hard greens that deflect even well-struck shots, and plenty of glimpses of Mount Bachelor and other peaks. The ninth hole is almost too beautiful to leave—a harmony of grasses, river, mountains, and trees that will leave your knees weak. Number twelve is a dissonant 687 yards from the biggie tees with water the entire way on the left side. The back has an opus of wonderful solos and not a sour note, but no easy riffs either. Sometimes you'll be glad to find a bunker that protected you from a worse fate.

Just when the buzz over Crosswater finally began settling down to

Meadow Lakes:
Prineville, Oregon ▶

a steady, musical hum, the resort added a new log to the crackling fire of golf excellence. In entirely redesigning Sunriver's **MEADOWS** golf course, architect John Fought took a page from the game's great golf course architects of the 1920s and 1930s—Alistair McKenzie, Donald Ross, and H. Chandler Egan—and suggested that while the meek might inherit the earth, they could no longer count on tearing up the Meadows course. In turning the lovely and friendly but formerly undistinguished Meadows into a modern classic stretching to

◀ Black Butte: Black Butte Ranch, Oregon

7,012 yards, Fought relied on elements of style employed by these legendary designers of that earlier time. In particular, Fought's use of faced bunkers, directional bunkers, and other visually stunning techniques has transformed the Meadows into a real player's course.

After frolicking through the new Meadows, graduate to the slightly more serious but equally fun **WOODLANDS** course, designed by Robert Trent Jones Jr. At 6,880 yards, this traditional venue is chock full of lakes, deep bunkers, and elevated greens. While not flashy, Woodlands reveals subtle, well-thought intricacies. It's like a Stickley table: solid, well-made, and a little old fashioned, as it was designed before playing from the tips became a macho test of endurance. Plenty of tight chipping areas around the greens heighten the challenge, and the fabulous finishing hole leaves a choice between hitting across a hairpin turn over a lake or knocking a long, straight iron to a safer but far more distant landing area.

Of course, there's plenty more to Sunriver than golf—namely bike trails, stables, a marina, tennis, a nature center, a spa, fishing, and a raft of other action sports (including rafting). And the resort offers condos and hotel rooms that will make you feel like you're an integral part of this grand and welcoming community. Which you'll need to be to have playing privileges at Crosswater. Which I'd sleep in a

◀ *Crosswater course
at Sunriver Resort:
Sunriver, Oregon*

bunker for, if I had to. But you should sleep in the fabulous River Lodges. These boldly muscular lodgings overlook the Meadows course and provide a level of luxury that will make you feel deliciously guilty.

Around the Bend area, a handful of other courses and resorts merit mentioning. Boasting more previous owners than the Amityville Horror, the Robert Muir Graves–designed **WIDGI CREEK GOLF CLUB** has finally stabilized as a dependable semiprivate course. Nine lakes and occasional dead trees add a dash of Graves character to the layout. The **RIVER'S EDGE GOLF COURSE**, affiliated with the Riverhouse Resort, offers an opportunity to get up and down on nearly every hole, because of the severe elevation changes. The layout requires some daring blind shots and masterful course management. One of my favorite-named golf courses anywhere, **LOST TRACKS GOLF CLUB** (implying someone hit a tee shot so far into the tullies that even his tracks disappeared) offers 7,003 yards of Brian Whitcomb–designed golf with lava rock rough and an island par 3 hole that you reach by crossing a bridge made from a railroad car. The course borders on the Deschutes National Forest. Prineville's **MEADOW LAKES GOLF COURSE** was one of the first designs to win *Golf Digest's* National Environmental Leaders award. This 6,731-yard bargain sculpted by William Bell offers at least eighteen chances to hit into water. Finally, the **PRONGHORN GOLF CLUB'S JACK NICKLAUS GOLF COURSE** will open for public play when the resort opens for public sleeping sometime in 2004. Pronghorn promises to be one of the most exciting developments in the area since the last volcanic eruption.

Should you lose your senses and tire of golfing in Central Oregon (or run out of balls), the area offers a dizzying array of other I-N-G sports, including hiking, biking, rafting, and fly-fishing. Hire a licensed guide to regale you with fish stories and teach you how to attract trout on the Deschutes River. The Paulina Plunge is all down-hill—from six thousand feet up on the edge of the caldera at New-berry Volcanic National Monument—on a mountain bike. Tours include lunch, short side hikes, and swimming in several waterfalls and natural water slides. Downtown Bend also features an artsy river walk with great galleries and shops, such as the Mirror Pond Gallery. And don't miss a visit to the High Desert Museum three miles south of town on U.S. 97.

In the high desert east of the Cascade Mountains, ride on toward the Native American–owned **WILDHORSE RESORT AND CASINO**, located just outside Pendleton. Wildhorse isn't a gamble at all: Lousy poker players will actually *make* money by paying the low greens fees on the golf course rather than betting their two pair against three of a kind. The underrated and largely unknown track stretches to 7,112 yards at the base of the Blue Mountains. Designed by local architect John Steidel, the holes wind across high plains amid native grasses beside fourteen hundred planted trees, including ponderosa pine, mountain mahogany, and western larch. On the horizon, view the Columbia Plateau, but also keep your eye on the greens, which slant and slope instead of undulating. The first good hole comes at number two, where two bunkers lurk in a hollow, OB (out of bounds) lies to the left, and the fairway curves uphill. The visuals here are tricky, making distances hard to figure. Other standouts include number fifteen, where a high mound hides the green and water waits patiently to the left. Along the course, you'll spot the Tamastslikt Cultural Institute, a Native American community center and museum well worth a visit following your round.

Also worth visiting is the high-desert western town of Pendleton. A century ago, the sleepy burg boasted thirty-two saloons and eighteen houses of ill repute. Today, it's most famous for the Round-Up, a rodeo that's taken place every September since 1910. If you miss the roping events, you can still visit the Hall of Fame Museum located under the grandstand. Downtown pick up the Pendleton Underground Tour, which proceeds through tunnels and subterranean rooms that once housed the Shamrock Card Room, a meat market, and a Chinese laundry. The rooms have been made to look as they did when in use, down to the smallest detail. Spend all your extra gold dust at the Pendleton Woolen Mills factory store.

ASPEN LAKES GOLF COURSE

16900 Aspen Lakes Drive, Sisters, OR 97759
541-549-4653 • www.aspenlakes.com
Architect/Years: William Overdorf, 1997, 2000
Tees/Yardages: 5 sets of tees from 5,594 to 7,302 yards
Season: March to November
Cost: $$ to $$$
Tee times: No restrictions

AWBREY GLEN GOLF CLUB

2500 NW Awbrey Glen Drive, Bend, OR 97701
541-388-8526 • www.awbreyglen.com
Architect/Year: Gene "Bunny" Mason, 1993
Tees/Yardages: 4 sets of tees from 5,396 to 7,029 yards
Season: March to November
Cost: $$$$
Tee times: Up to 6 days in advance

BLACK BUTTE RANCH

PO Box 8000, Black Butte Ranch, OR 97759
800-399-2322 • www.blackbutteranch.com

Glaze Meadow

Architect/Year: Gene "Bunny" Mason, 1982
Tees/Yardages: 3 sets of tees from 5,545 to 6,574 yards
Season: April to October
Cost: $$ to $$$
Tee times: Resort guests up to 45 days in advance, nonguests up to 30 days in advance

Big Meadow

Architect/Year: Robert Muir Graves, 1972
Tees/Yardages: 3 sets of tees from 5,679 to 6,850 yards
Season: April to October
Cost: $$ to $$$
Tee times: Resort guests up to 45 days in advance, nonguests up to 30 days in advance

BROKEN TOP CLUB

62000 Broken Top Drive, Bend, OR 97702
541-383-8200 • www.brokentop.com
Architects/Year: Tom Weiskopf and Jay Morrish, 1993
Tees/Yardages: 4 sets of tees from 5,281 to 7,165 yards
Season: March to November
Cost: $$$$$
Tee times: Up to 1 week in advance

EAGLE CREST RESORT

1522 Cline Falls Highway, Redmond, OR 97756
541-923-4653 • www.eagle-crest.com

Ridge Course

Architect/Year: John Thronson, 1994
Tees/Yardages: 5 sets of tees from 4,792 to 6,927 yards
Season: March to October, one course (alternates yearly) open all year
Cost: $ to $$$
Tee times: Resort guests up to 30 days in advance, nonguests up to 2 weeks in advance

Resort Course

Architect/Year: Gene "Bunny" Mason, 1986
Tees/Yardages: 2 sets of tees from 5,395 to 6,673 yards
Season: March to October, one course (alternates yearly) open all year
Cost: $ to $$$

Tee times: Resort guests up to 30 days in advance, nonguests up to 2 weeks in advance

Mid-Irons Course

Architect/Year: John Thronson, 2000
Tees/Yardages: 3 sets of tees from 2,982 to 4,160 yards
Season: March to October
Cost: $ to $$
Tee times: Resort guests up to 30 days in advance, nonguests up to 2 weeks in advance

LOST TRACKS GOLF CLUB

60205 Sunset View Drive, Bend, OR 97702
541-385-1818
Architect/Year: Brian Whitcomb, 1996
Tees/Yardages: 4 sets of tees from 5,287 to 7,003 yards
Season: Year-round
Cost: $$ to $$$
Tee times: Up to 2 weeks in advance

MEADOW LAKES GOLF COURSE

300 Meadow Lakes Drive, Prineville, OR 97754
800-577-2797 • www.cityofprineville.com
Architect/Year: Bill Robinson, 1993
Tees/Yardages: 4 sets of tees from 5,155 to 6,731 yards
Season: Year-round
Cost: $ to $$
Tee times: No restrictions, more than 1 week in advance must be held with credit card

PRONGHORN GOLF CLUB

830 NW Wall Street, Bend, OR 97701
800-541-9424 • www.pronghorngolfclub.com
Architect/Year: Jack Nicklaus, 2004
Tees/Yardages: NA
Season: NA
Cost: NA
Tee times: NA

RIVER'S EDGE GOLF COURSE/RIVERHOUSE RESORT

400 Pro Shop Drive, Bend, OR 97701
541-389-2828 • www.riverhouse.com
Architect/Year: Robert Muir Graves, 1987
Tees/Yardages: 4 sets of tees from 5,381 to 6,683 yards
Season: Year-round
Cost: $$ to $$$
Tee times: Up to 30 days in advance

SUNRIVER RESORT

1 Center Drive, Sunriver, OR 97707
800-547-3922 • www.sunriver-resort.com

Woodlands

Architect/Year: Robert Trent Jones Jr., 1981
Tees/Yardages: 3 sets of tees from 5,446 to 6,880 yards
Season: April to October
Cost: $$$ to $$$$$
Tee times: Resort guests no restrictions, nonguests up to 10 days in advance

Crosswater

Architecht/Year: Bob Cupp, 1995
Tees/Yardages: 5 sets of tees from 5,359 to 7,683 yards
Season: April to October
Cost: $$$$ to $$$$$
Tee times: Resort guests no restrictions, nonguests up to 10 days in advance

Meadows

Architect/Year: John Fought, 1999
Tees/Yardages: 4 sets of tees from 5,287 to 7,012 yards
Season: April to October
Cost: $$$ to $$$$$
Tee times: Resort guests no restrictions, nonguests up to 10 days in advance

WIDGI CREEK GOLF CLUB

18707 SW Century Drive, Bend, OR 97702
541-382-4449 • www.widgi.com
Architect/Year: Robert Muir Graves, 1991
Tees/Yardages: 4 sets of tees from 5,070 to 6,903 yards
Season: March to November
Cost: $ to $$$
Tee times: Up to 1 month in advance

WILDHORSE RESORT AND CASINO

72777 Highway 331, Pendleton, OR 97801
800-654-9453 • www.wildhorseresort.com
Architect/Year: John Steidel, 1997
Tees/Yardages: 4 sets of tees from 5,718 to 7,112 yards
Season: March to October
Cost: $$
Tee times: Up to 30 days in advance

59

SOUTHERN OREGON

LOCATED ON THE DRY SIDE of Oregon's Cascade Mountains halfway between San Francisco and Portland, the RUNNING Y RANCH RESORT hunkers between ponderosa forests, towering fault blocks, slumbering volcanoes, lava formations, and thirty-mile Klamath Lake. Nobody will ask you to rope a stray heifer at the Running Y, although several thousand acres of the resort still operate as an active ranch. But you can still go horseback riding— or mountain biking, canoeing, hiking, or work out in the fitness center, or simply sit for a spell, absorbing expansive views from an Adirondack chair on the back porch of the lodge.

Outside, the resort's architecture and personality holler pure Wild West. Buildings were modeled

◀ *Running Y Ranch: Klamath Falls, Oregon*

after local historical structures, blending ranch and Craftsman styles. The golf clubhouse, characterized by open trusses and high ceilings, suggests the kind of big-fisted ranch home that might have occupied the property a hundred years ago. The area around the resort was traditionally home to ranchers and loggers, and in earlier times golf might have figured in the punch lines of many hilarious workingman's jokes here. Nobody's laughing anymore. In fact, as Oregon's timber economy has suffered in recent years, tree wood has given way to three-woods as a major source of revenue.

Although the Y's golf course corralled Arnold Palmer's moniker, builder John Thronson was largely responsible for the creative design and for the moundings that correspond to the shapes of distant hills and peaks. The layout provides eighteen good reasons for visiting the resort. It stretches 7,133 yards from the black Palmer tees, but a mere 5,977 from the whites, and plays even shorter due to the altitude.

Tees and rough are edged with perky fescues, and the Bentgrass fairways undulate pleasantly. The course is really a sampler plate of golfing delicacies: The first four holes tease along the edge of Klamath Lake and marshes aflap with birds and waterfowl (the resort stretches along the Pacific flyway, so visitors include herons, bald eagles, and tundra swans). The first few greens are deep and narrow and require fluffy wedge shots over ponds and white sands. The signature par-3 fifth, at 158 yards, blends fresh design elements into a delicious stew: rocks behind the green that mirror distant, rocky hills; trees to the left that presage a transition into forest; and long, serene views of Klamath Lake. Following number five, the layout climbs onto a tree-lined plateau, lending it a muscular, timbery Northwest feel. The toughest hole may be number six, a long par 4 with a sloping, misanthropic green that tilts from left to right.

The back side begins in open meadows punctuated by lakes and scooped mounds. After the steeply downhill par-3 twelfth, the course disappears into sage-scented, creek-lined Payne Canyon. It pokes out into the open again at seventeen, a par 5 that plays along two separate fairways divided by a pine tree. Choose the upper landing area to earn a second shot at the green. Overall, the layout is short but wonderfully strategic, and the scenery and rugged outdoor feel will have you tossing your ten-gallon golf cap in the air and yelling "Yee-haw, little doggy!" as your ball rolls toward the cup.

The Running Y Ranch Lodge features woodsy Northwest cowboy décor—just remove your chaps before entering the restaurant. Non-golf diversions include side trips to Crater Lake National Park and the world-renowned Shakespeare Festival in Ashland.

Not far from the Running Y lies daily-fee **EAGLE POINT GOLF CLUB**, designed by Robert Trent Jones Jr. From terrain that rolls gently through meadows crossed by streams, this 7,099-yard layout offers views of 9,495-foot Mount McLoughlin, the Table Rocks, and a number of volcanic peaks. Sand is visible as well, in the form of strategic and directional bunkers. Thanks to masterful drainage techniques and fairways that were veneered with six inches of sand, this incredible golf value is open for play all year.

As it moves through its pastoral setting, Eagle Point provides a collection of optical challenges, such as bunkers that appear to hug the greens but actually lie much farther out. Four sets of tees and large putting surfaces lend further character. The front nine routes clockwise through a flat, open plain; the back side encompasses a number of elevation changes.

The 580-yard fourth hole is made easier than it sounds with the help of a prevailing wind and by avoiding the central fairway bunker. The 471-yard sixth is possibly the most difficult, serving up a three-course meal of length, water, and sand. Several tee shots at Eagle Point—including the one on the 591-yard sixteenth—play directly at Mount McLoughlin.

Eagle Point Golf Club:
Eagle Point, Oregon ▶

EAGLE POINT GOLF CLUB

100 Eagle Point Drive, Eagle Point, OR 97524
541-826-8225 • www.eaglepointgolf.com
Architect/Year: Robert Trent Jones Jr., 1996
Tees/Yardages: 4 sets of tees from 5,071 to 7,099 yards
Season: Year-round
Cost: $ to $$$
Tee times: Up to 2 weeks in advance, no restrictions if held with credit card

RUNNING Y RANCH RESORT

5790 Coopers Hawk, Klamath Falls, OR 97601
888-850-0261 • www.runningy.com
Architect/Year: Arnold Palmer, 1998
Tees/Yardages: 5 sets of tees from 4,842 to 7,133 yards
Season: Year-round
Cost: $$ to $$$
Tee times: Resort guests no restrictions, nonguests up to 2 weeks in advance

SEATTLE AND ENVIRONS

IF YOU HOPE to find a place around Seattle that does not have a Starbucks, you can (a) swim out into Puget Sound (not even Seattle's ferry system, the largest in the United States, is latte free) or (b) go play golf (you should be safe once you leave the clubhouse, as long as no beverage cart is in sight).

The city that transformed coffee into a lifestyle choice is largely fueled by hip, entrepreneurial individualists (think Microsoft and Amazon) who love the outdoors, religiously follow the Mariners, work to protect the environment, and consume their body weight in espresso drinks daily.

The character of a city as creative and eclectic as Seattle is hard to define, although water defines it topographically—not only the Sound, but Lakes

◀ The Golf Club at Newcastle's Coal Creek Course: Newcastle, Washington

Washington and Union, which all help to create the maritime feeling of the place. Boats leave downtown Seattle for ports as close as the recreationally rich San Juan Islands and as distant as Vancouver, British Columbia, and Alaska. Beyond the rim of downtown, orient yourself by looking for the Space Needle (remnant of the 1962 World's Fair) to the north, Mount Rainier and the Cascade Mountains to the east, and the Olympic Range across the Sound to the west. On a clear day (read: summer), few urban areas offer a more impressive view.

One of six cities nationwide with a symphony, opera, and ballet in residence, visual arts also express local angst and joy on everything from bus tunnels to manhole covers. A love of music and architecture drove Microsoft billionaire Paul Allen to commission Frank Gehry to design a three-story, guitar-shaped building called the Experience Music Project, an overcaffeinated museum and interactive space. Residents of this always green city boast the highest percentage of college degrees and more two-wheeled commuters than any other U.S. metropolis, but actually less rain falls here than in Miami or New York—though it falls slowly, over a long period of time (namely, every day in winter).

Although Seattle is a city of neighborhoods, such as funky Fremont, elegant Queen Anne, and trendy Belltown, downtown hops, too. It's home to Safeco Field and Seahawks Stadium, as well as what may be the world's best bookstore (Elliott Bay Books). Locals and visitors alike crowd Pike Place Market, the oldest continually working farmers market, not only to shop for the freshest seafood, baked goods, and produce but also to buy crafts, watch street performers, and see fishmongers hurl giant salmon at each other. Downtown is also a traveler's city, with hotels such as the sleek and hip W and the smart and artsy Elliott Grand Hyatt, which earned a designation as a Leading Hotel of the World before it even opened. For creatively

Gold Mountain's Olympic Course: Bremerton, Washington ▶

prepared cuisine, try Restaurant Zoe or Flying Fish. The latter, staffed by a bunch of renegade golfers, serves up a stunning variety of fish species, all caught wild rather than farm raised. Chef/owner Christine Keff provides a dining room as lively as her food is unique.

Golfers worldwide turned toward Seattle in 1998 to watch the PGA Championship played at the Redmond neighborhood's Sahalee Golf Club. But the city by the Sound has not caught on as a great golf destination despite a glittering collection of deep green venues located within striking distance of the downtown core. Seattle's golf is dispersed among islands and peninsulas and suburban neighborhoods, although downtown still makes for a perfect base of operations to take in all of the local charms, golf-related and otherwise.

The golf venue located closest to downtown may just be one of the world's best urban munis. **WEST SEATTLE GOLF COURSE** is set in an old neighborhood filled with Craftsman-style homes just across the West Seattle Bridge. The layout was designed by renowned course architect H. Chandler Egan in 1939. Egan performed some of his most memorable work on Pebble Beach Golf Links, though he is seldom credited for it. Built on the side of a hill and winding amid steep ravines and towering firs overlooking downtown's modern skyline, West Seattle's dramatic 6,623-yard track may lack an ocean but there's not a bad hole on the course. It hosted the 1953 Public Links Championship and annually hosts the final round of the Seattle Men's Amateur Championship.

West Seattle's views—and fairways—are generous, although its greens prove more, how shall we say, economical (okay, they're downright stingy), at least from the perspective of size. The second hole offers a startling glimpse of the Space Needle; this 346-yarder follows the scalloped edges of a stream bank on the right without leaving much space for drives that don't thread the needle. Number three, also short, is also perfectly sculpted, a 121-yard par 3 routed over a clear stream at the bottom of a ravine that must be carried. The front side includes three par 5s that never feel overly long but are always challenging. The twelfth hole presents a raucous par 5 that flows down in tiers for 515 yards before climbing back up to an elevated green. The layout includes fewer than a dozen bunkers—the real challenge is designed into the use of ravines, difficult lies, and demanding green complexes.

Half an hour from Seattle—and perched on a hill that sometimes sits above the fog that envelops downtown—is **THE GOLF CLUB AT NEWCASTLE**, built with the vision (and money) of former Microsoft executive Scott Oki. The operating system in force at Newcastle is impeccable service

(such as heated toilet seats in the restrooms) amid unimaginable views. From the moment you crest the hill at this startling complex, you'll be overwhelmed by the high quality of everything from the stone clubhouse to the warmly paneled restaurant, from the putting course to the snack house, which features a dozen varieties of mustard to slather on your hot dog. Fred Couples teamed up with Bob Cupp to design two layouts here. In addition to glimpses of downtown, Puget Sound, Mount Rainier, and the Olympic Mountains vie for attention.

You'd also best pay attention to the golf terrain—both courses at Newcastle feature a number of holes lent goofiness by the difficult topography. Greens, for example, are hilariously fast when your opponent is putting but downright frightening when it's your turn. Essentially built on the side of a mountain, these target venues require you to think ahead and figure where to land shots so they kick toward fairways and greens. They may also require a sense of humor. As if the steep gains and drops in elevation don't make club selection hard enough, many of the green fronts are built to deflect approach shots back down hills.

The first Cupp/Couples coupling here, **COAL CREEK**, stretches 7,024 yards and offers up five par 3s and five par 5s. Two of the best holes

◀ *Trophy Lake:*
Port Orchard, Washington

open the back nine. Number ten is a 226-yard downhill odyssey that makes club selection an educated guess. Number eleven, a 547-yard double dogleg, features an extremely narrow fairway with a steep hillside to the right, a bunker guarding the fairway on the second shot, and a narrow green hanging on the edge of a precipice. Number eighteen, a wide, windy uphill journey, feels almost Scottish, and the waiting clubhouse—44,000 square feet of cultured stone, copper, granite, tile, and wood trim—creates the feel of a nineteenth-century British manor. Don't miss the Wooly Toad Cigar Bar upstairs. The second course at Newcastle, **CHINA CREEK**, plays to 6,676 yards and a par of 71. It is similar in design, style, and opulent service to Coal Creek.

Forty minutes south of Seattle, in Auburn, architect John Fought designed an exciting syllabus for **WASHINGTON NATIONAL GOLF CLUB**, a facility with a University of Washington theme. Players who like to go to school on their partners' putts may start humming "Pomp and Circumstance" on Fought's 7,304-yard layout, which promises to test your golf faculties. The UW colors of purple and gold adorn everything from flags to staff uniforms, and every purple-trimmed golf cart is named for a former Husky sports legend. A number of other carts are decorated with the logos of other PAC-10 schools. All Washington

National buildings replicate famous structures from the UW campus, including grandstand seating around the eighteenth green that recalls Husky stadium. The UW men's and women's golf teams use Washington National as their practice site and home course.

In the hopes of attracting a U.S. Open to the venue, Fought incorporated features from some of the world's best layouts: diagonal shot qualities and mounded greens similar to Augusta National; bunker styles that recall Riviera and Winged Foot; natural dunesy waste areas like those at Pine Valley; and humongous putting

Washington National:
Auburn, Washington ▶

surfaces that emulate Oakmont. Like many Open venues, the course also includes four exceptionally long par 4s—such as number eighteen, which plays 475 yards over wastelands and a fronting bunker to a green as large as some campus quads.

Fought may well possess a master of arts in waste areas—here, in addition to very ample free-form bunkering, the architect incorporated scads of long, sandy swaths containing coarse sand speckled with natural vegetation. One such area actually encompasses white sand bunker islands within the darker sand. Holes fifteen through seventeen of the **UNIVERSITY COURSE** are its real highlight; a rollicking lake and stream complex wends around greens and fairways and must have been inspired by input from the drama department. Unfortunately for high-handicappers, scores at Washington National are not graded on a curve.

The **PORT LUDLOW GOLF COURSE**, reachable on the Olympic Peninsula via ferry or roundabout drive from Seattle, encompasses three nines that are all tens if you love rugged scenic beauty, wild native grasses, gazillions of wildflowers that run amok, and the kind of golf challenge that will have you cursing and caressing your clubs like some crazed S&M freak who's consumed one too many cocktails. The longest, toughest eighteen holes here play to just under 6,800 yards.

Architect Robert Muir Graves knocked Ludlow's original course (Tide/Timber) out of second-growth forest in 1975. Timber barons/resort developers Pope and Talbot had already decimated the original old-growth forests on much of Washington's Olympic Peninsula outside of nearby Olympic National Park, and Graves left many root fans and humongous cedar stumps in place along the golf course as a sort of haunting testimony to the ancient trees. The remnants also work as lovely modernist decoration and occasionally make for an amusing lie (as long as it's your friend's ball that somehow ends up inside a stump).

The **TIDE** nine is the easiest and least dramatic of the three, wandering between lakes and streams and a few bail-out areas. The second hole, a 320-yard par 4, drops precipitously enough to require a tee-side periscope to reveal whether the group in front of you is finished and that no enemy subs are approaching. The tee offers expansive views of Ludlow Bay and snowy mountains beyond.

The **TIMBER** nine is tighter, tougher, and quieter, tunneling through thick woods and creating an achingly remote and reverential atmosphere. Things open up a little on the eighth, a par 3 that ranges from 128 to 171 yards from six different tees. Here, you can actually see other holes, feel the joy of community, smell fragrant cedar smoke and the salt breeze off the bay; you can relax, until you notice that the hole demands an accurate shot over a giant lake surrounded by cedar stumps.

The **TRAIL** nine, also designed by Graves, opened in 1992 and then again in 1993 after a few sniveling members insisted the architect make it easier. Trail is still the toughest and most scenic of the triumvirate, verging on target golf and featuring several forced carries over ravines and wetlands with alders and firs closing in from the sides. Speaking of wet, it's got water on eight holes. Number three

◀ *Druid's Glen: Covington, Washington*

requires a tee shot layup to avoid rolling down a steep hill into a ravine and a second layup in front of a water hazard. At 465 downhill yards from the whites, this par-5 temptress may require a lot of balls.

The golf course is associated with the Inn at Port Ludlow, a soft-spoken compendium of airy rooms resting on a spit overlooking the water, with *ooh/aah* views of the Olympic and Cascade Mountains. Outside, clapboard siding, weathered cedar shingles, and a wrap-around porch chaired by wicker rockers make for the perfect place to set a while. Inside, the inn blends a sort of East Coast Brahman beachiness, rugged Northwest bravado, and Tribeca chic.

Think of the one-hour Seattle to Bremerton ferry as a caddie for your car. Or make the comparable drive to this peninsula off the east side of the Olympic Peninsula to reach three of the Seattle area's finest golf venues.

First stop, **TROPHY LAKE GOLF AND CASTING** in Port Orchard. As you might guess from its name, Trophy Lake combines golf with fishing—a perfect pairing as many players will be fishing for golf balls and should also be careful with their hooks. Even the score card at Trophy Lake says, "Golf balls and fish are catch and release only." Architect John Fought has crafted a fabulous, smart, and daring risk/reward golf experience with sloping fairways, expansive greens,

79

and eighty deep-faced bunkers winking across the 7,206-yard track. The drama is heightened by a number of split and tiered fairways and severe drop-offs into thick forests of fir. The 547-yard finishing hole is bordered by a water feature that is also full of giant trout and steelhead that have grown bold on their balata diet; hence they can swim with backspin.

Also in Port Orchard lies THE GOLF COURSE AT MCCORMICK WOODS. This twenty-four-year-old Jack Frei design has won its share of "bests" over the years—and for good reason. For starters, no adjoining fairways will distract you with golfers kicking their bags and cursing at the innocent trees. Five elevated tees on each hole provide perfect stages for hitting between ponds, lakes, pines, and firs and across sloping terrain. Plenty of OB throughout and views of Mount Rainier from the twelfth tee will add to the excitement. The course plays to 7,040 yards with large greens sporting gentle contours. Knowing the yardages to the hazards will help to keep you from, for example, poking your drive more than 242 yards into the bunker on number twelve. Have your birding life list handy for when you spot yellow warblers, purple finches, or hairy woodpeckers.

Close by to the Port Orchard golf courses, in nearby Bremerton, lies the GOLD MOUNTAIN GOLF COMPLEX, a fabulous pair of municipal

Port Ludlow: Port Ludlow, Washington ▶

courses run with Swiss precision and exuding the active feel of a popular private club. The courses have a reputation for draining well and thus offer some of the best winter conditions, which is saying something in the Northwest. The courses are carved from Olympic Peninsula forests, and the watershed status of the land ensures that no homesites or development will mar the natural setting.

Jack Reimer designed Gold Mountain's **CASCADE COURSE** in 1971. This well-rated 6,707-yard venue boasts wooded enclaves, rolling terrain, wide fairways, and fast, well-bunkered greens. But the highlight at Gold Mountain is a course named for the other local mountain range: the **OLYMPIC COURSE**, John Harbottle's excellent 1996 effort, which stretches to 7,035 yards. Wide ryegrass fairways, fescue rough, and five water holes characterize this venue that *GOLF Magazine* named among its top-ten best new public courses in 1997. Sculpted angles and narrow mowing patterns on the fairways are just part of the story here, as are tee shots hit into upslopes that often work to kill distance. The fifth hole offers a lovely snapshot of Harbottle's artistry: Pot bunkers along the left side of this 528-yard par 5 reflect opposite mirror images of mounds on the right side. The seventeenth is one of the best here, a massive 467-yard par 4 with wetlands and tall, skinny trees along the left side, water right, and a long carry to the green. The eighteenth offers a strange and daring finish: a 305-yard par 4 that encourages you to attack the green over a battlefield of pot bunkers, trees, and waste areas—or take the pussy-boy route with an iron to the curving fairway.

Druids were the intellectual poet-philosophers of ancient Ireland, and glens were where they came together to share experiences. So it is with golfers who trek to Kent, forty minutes from Seattle, to discuss golf philosophy at **DRUID'S GLEN GOLF CLUB**. The 7,146 yards and invigorating treks between some holes provide lots of time to philosophize as you wander across Bentgrass through second-growth forest beside sixty bunkers and nine lakes. Keith Foster is the Druid architect, and his specialty is definitely par 3s, which are excellent here. The first requires a flight over water to a small green. The biggest treat comes on a handful of isolated holes on the back nine that lend a wilderness feeling. Number fourteen is a fine 522-yard par 5 with a wetland island dividing the fairway.

Two more courses fill out the Seattle golf dance card. **HARBOUR POINTE GOLF CLUB** in Mukilteo, fifteen miles from Seattle, presents a 6,861-yard Arthur Hills design with water on the first ten holes. Number two plays between two separate lakes as it winds 444 yards from tee to green. The sixth hole, at 509 yards, features a lake along the entire right side, except where a bunker comes between the fairway and the lake. **KAYAK POINT GOLF COURSE** in Stanwood has been serving Seattle's public golfers proudly since 1977. The 6,719-yard Ron Fream design is managed by Arnold Palmer Golf Management, though you probably won't see Arnie working in the bag room. In spite of its location—and name—Kayak has virtually no water; if you hit into any, you may have made a wrong turn. Rolling hills and elevation changes provide part of the challenge here, but a few million board feet of timber get into the act, as well. The ninth hole is one of the best—a 505-yard double dogleg with a tree island to negotiate on the approach. Number fourteen features a split fairway that could divide, but ultimately reunite, friends and family.

If you're planning on playing even half of the great golf courses in the Seattle area during one visit, I recommend a triple mocha latte at least three times a day.

DRUID'S GLEN GOLF CLUB

29925 207th Avenue SE, Covington, WA 98042
253-638-1200 • www.druidsglengolf.com
Architect/Year: Keith Foster, 1997
Tees/Yardages: 4 sets of tees from 5,354 to 7,146 yards
Season: Year-round
Cost: $$ to $$$
Tee times: Up to 1 week in advance

GOLD MOUNTAIN GOLF COMPLEX

7263 W Belfair Valley Road, Bremerton, WA 98312
360-415-5432 • www.goldmt.com

Olympic Course

Architect/Year: John Harbottle, 1996
Tees/Yardages: 4 sets of tees from 5,220 to 7,035 yards
Season: Year-round
Cost: $ to $$
Tee times: Up to 30 days in advance

Cascade Course

Architect/Year: Jack Reimer, 1971
Tees/Yardages: 4 sets of tees from 5,306 to 6,707 yards
Season: Year-round
Cost: $ to $$
Tee times: Up to 30 days in advance

THE GOLF CLUB AT NEWCASTLE

15500 Six Penny Lane, Newcastle, WA 98059
425-793-5566 • www.newcastlegolf.com

Coal Creek

Architects/Year: Bob Cupp with Billy Fuller and Fred Couples, 1999
Tees/Yardages: 4 sets of tees from 5,153 to 7,024 yards
Season: Year-round
Cost: $$$$$
Tee times: Up to 1 week in advance

China Creek

Architects/Year: Bob Cupp with Billy Fuller and Fred Couples, 2001
Tees/Yardages: 4 sets of tees from 4,566 to 6,676 yards
Season: Year-round
Cost: $$$ to $$$$
Tee times: Up to 1 week in advance

THE GOLF COURSE AT MCCORMICK WOODS

5155 McCormick Woods Drive SW, Port Orchard, WA 98367
800-323-0130 • www.mccormickwoodsgolf.com
Architect/Year: Jack Frei, 1986
Tees/Yardages: 5 sets of tees from 5,299 to 7,040 yards
Season: Year-round
Cost: $ to $$
Tee times: Up to 1 week in advance, groups of 20 or more up to 30 days in advance

HARBOUR POINTE GOLF CLUB

11817 Harbour Pointe Boulevard, Mukilteo, WA 98275
800-233-3128 • www.harbourpointe.com
Architect/Year: Arthur Hills, 1990
Tees/Yardages: 5 sets of tees from 4,836 to 6,861 yards
Season: Year-round
Cost: $$ to $$$
Tee times: Up to 1 week in advance

KAYAK POINT GOLF COURSE

15711 Marine Drive, Stanwood, WA 98292
800-562-3094 • www.kayakpoint.com
Architect/Year: Ron Fream, 1977
Tees/Yardages: 3 sets of tees from 5,332 to 6,719 yards
Season: Year-round
Cost: $ to $$
Tee times: Up to 2 weeks in advance

PORT LUDLOW GOLF COURSE

751 Highland Drive, Port Ludlow, WA 98365
800-455-0272 • www.ludlowbayresort.com

Timber (nine holes)

Architect/Year: Robert Muir Graves, 1975
Tees/Yardages: 4 sets of tees from 2,759 to 3,430 yards
Season: Year-round
Cost: $$ to $$$
Tee times: Inn guests no restrictions, nonguests up to 2
weeks in advance

Trail (nine holes)

Architect/Year: Robert Muir Graves, 1992
Tees/Yardages: 4 sets of tees from 2,353 to 3,326 yards
Season: Year-round
Cost: $$ to $$$
Tee times: Inn guests no restrictions, nonguests up to 2
weeks in advance

Tide (nine holes)

Architect/Year: Robert Muir Graves, 1975
Tees/Yardages: 4 sets of tees from 2,839 to 3,357 yards
Season: Year-round
Cost: $$ to $$$
Tee times: Inn guests no restrictions, nonguests up to 2
weeks in advance

TROPHY LAKE GOLF AND CASTING

3900 SW Lake Flora Road, Port Orchard, WA 98367
360-874-8337 • www.trophylakegolfclub.com
Architect/Year: John Fought, 1999
Tees/Yardages: 5 sets of tees from 5,342 to 7,206 yards
Season: Year-round
Cost: $$ to $$$
Tee times: Up to 30 days in advance

WASHINGTON NATIONAL GOLF CLUB

14330 SE Husky Way, Auburn, WA 98092
253-333-5000 • www.washingtonnationalgolfclub.com
Architect/Year: John Fought, 2000
Tees/Yardages: 5 sets of tees from 5,117 to 7,304 yards
Season: Year-round
Cost: $$ to $$$$
Tee times: Up to 30 days in advance

WEST SEATTLE GOLF COURSE

4470 35th Avenue SW, Seattle, WA 98126
206-935-5187 • www.westseattlegolf.com
Architect/Year: H. Chandler Egan, 1940
Tees/Yardages: 3 sets of tees from 5,611to 6,623 yards
Season: Year-round
Cost: $ to $$
Tee times: Up to 1 week in advance

NORTH PUGET SOUND

THE SEMIAHMOO RESORT IN BLAINE, Washington, was named after a local Indian leader who reportedly paid ten blankets for the moniker to a Northwest Coast tribal chief. The resort spreads leisurely across a long spit of sand that reaches into a calm bay. Semiahmoo's stately timber-and-stone inn offers views of both the Cascade Mountains and the glimmering lights of Victoria, British Columbia, across the water, where descendants of a certain chief shall remain nameless.

According to a brochure produced by the resort, it takes twenty-four hours to reach the property from Seattle by balloon, twelve hours by inline skating, and only six minutes by skydiving. The two-and-a-half hours by car pass quickly, too. Whatever mode of

◄ *Semiahmoo: Blaine, Washington*

89

transport you choose, the point is to hurry: The faster you arrive, the sooner you'll be able to kick back and enjoy the very best the Northwest has to offer. Admire the scenery from the inn's lobby espresso bar, the oyster bar, or the sand bar out back. The manly, elegant, woodsy facility is chock full of picture windows, fireplaces, intimate libraries, leather chairs, and a soothing sense of quiet.

Or view the scenery from your own airy guest room full of pine and bookshelves, desks and easy chairs, a large fluffy bed with down pillows, and perhaps even a fireplace to help you attain maximum coziness on the cold, damp nights that are prevalent in this climate. Lying on the bed in my own room, I picked up a remote control from the night table and aimed it at the television but heard only a whirring sound. Then I noticed that above me an electric shade was retracting to reveal a skylight. You'll want to spend a lot of time in your room, except that so darn many other things will tempt you away—such as a visit to the world-class health club and spa, which offer all the face scrubs, mud masks, and massages imaginable, as well as an indoor track, squash courts, and other surprising amenities—in addition to all the requisite ones (a pool, tennis courts, weights, etc.). Or head out to the marina, a nearby park, or the croquet greensward located between the inn and the bay.

One hundred years ago, the Pacific Star Fleet delivered salmon from the cannery located on the current site of the resort to cities up and down the Pacific coast. Today, Stars Restaurant delivers salmon, as well: I recommend one grilled on an alder plank and served with tiny, delicate vegetables and accompanied by a round of oysters on the half shell still tasting of the sea. You can eat while watching sunset over the bay.

You'll also satisfy your appetite for golf at Semiahmoo. The resort's two courses were ranked numbers one and two in the state by *Golf Digest*. The Palmer/Seay–designed **SEMIAHMOO GOLF AND COUNTRY CLUB** course seems as spacious as the rooms at the inn and as wide as it is long. Beautifully contoured fairways wind curvily for just over 7,000 yards from the back tees. More than fifty amoeba-shaped white sandpits threaten to engulf errant shots and call for accurate play close in to the big, rolling greens, which generally slope from side to side, back to front, front to back, or all of the above: The course doesn't contain a straight line anywhere. The routing tours through cedars and firs, lakes and wildflowers, and it offers mountain and bay views.

Semiahmoo's golf exudes a neat, well-coifed feel, but it's also a good-enough layout to have drawn a U.S. Amateur qualifying round in 1996 and a U.S. Open qualifying round the following year.

Houses abound, but they're set back far enough to allow for a sense of space.

The course opens with a dogleg-left par 5 of 491 yards that sets the scene well: Ten more doglegs follow. As on many of the holes here, a directional fairway bunker draws your eye toward the best target, especially if you can take that line and draw your shot into the dogleg a bit. The 412-yard second hole gives slicers an even chance as it doglegs in the opposite direction. Keep an eye out for the eagle living in a grand fir on the left side.

Number eighteen, which frames the clubhouse, is Semiahmoo's full ah-moo! Five fairway bunkers and three greenside beaches (one with a cedar tree growing out of it); water in front, right, and back; and the anticipation of the comfort of the awaiting inn all stack up to make this a tough 409-yard finish.

Guests at the inn (and the general public) can also play the formerly private **LOOMIS TRAIL GOLF CLUB**, designed by talented Canadian designer Graham Cooke. The course's fast greens have helped it earn the second-highest slope rating in the state (145). Of course, water on every hole probably contributed. The Bentgrass fairways are renowned for draining well; ideally, you'll be known for doing the same thing when putting. The links-style layout is very different from the Semiahmoo Golf and Country Club course and is still hous-ing-free. Great holes here include number two, a boomeranging 562-yard par 5 with two lakes, and the par-5 eleventh (506 yards), which offers an alternative fairway that cuts a significant amount of distance off the hole but requires precise shot making around water and sand.

Semiahmoo is also located within driving distance of the perky college town of Bellingham, home to Western Washington University. *Golf Digest*, which never encountered a golf course,

Homestead Farms:
Lynden, Washington ▶

93

town, cocktail, shoelace, or anything else it didn't love, once called Bellingham the seventh-best little golf town in America, whatever that means.

Plenty of other publications have had equally nice things to say. *Outside Magazine* called Bellingham one of the top-ten dream towns for working and playing. *Kiplinger's* considered it one of the best cities in which to retire. Bellingham has also ranked among the top-twenty cities in the United States if you happen to like clean air.

Attractions here include Pioneer Park, which houses a fine collection of log houses and artifacts, and the historic Fairhaven district, home to the most awesome Village Books. Whale watch from Point Roberts (or be watched by the whales), hike, kayak, visit wineries, disappear into the remote North Cascade Mountains, or snowboard on Mount Baker, which set a record in 1999 when it accumulated 1,140 inches of snow.

Of course, you can golf here, too. Fourteen courses weigh in close by, at least four of which merit driving to from your cozy digs at Semiahmoo or staying in town for a couple of nights.

SHUKSAN GOLF CLUB has its ups and downs—literally. Elevation changes of as much as 150 feet will make your golf ball think it just finished riding the Cyclone—if it survives the round, that is. Thick

second-cut and scary-thick rough beyond that may provide said
Titleist with enough cover to hide from you and return to the wild.
Creeks, ponds, wetlands, and sidehill lies may conspire to help your
ball disappear. The Rick Dvorak design stretches to 6,774 yards,
much of it in the Scottish links style.

The **LAKE PADDEN MUNICIPAL GOLF COURSE**, dreamed up by the architectural alliance of Roy Goss and Glen Proctor, challenged participants in the PGA Public Links Championship in 1995. Now it's
waiting for you to take on its narrow, isolated, tree-lined fairways.
Just remember to tell your loved ones where you're headed before
venturing out on this challenging track of 6,575 yards.

If we're voting on golf courses with evocative names, how about a
few ballots for **SUDDEN VALLEY GOLF AND COUNTRY CLUB**, whose
moniker suggests that at one moment there was flat land here and
the next—*whoa!* This semiprivate Ted Robinson design features a
watery front and a narrow, hilly "behind" nine, not to mention startling views of Lake Whatcom and the Stewart Mountains if you suddenly look up from your puny drive. The course plays to 6,553 yards.

Rounding out the rollicking rota of golf in the upper left corner of
the upper-leftist state of Washington is **HOMESTEAD FARMS GOLF
RESORT**. The year-round venue boasts the only par 5 played to an

island green in the entire state—possibly in the known universe (okay, maybe not). If Bill Overdorf's seven-thousand-plus yards prove too much, why not work on your short game on the eighteen-hole putting course?

An added benefit of playing any of the courses around Semiahmoo or Bellingham is that you're close to the Canadian border if you need to make a run for it after winning a dangerous local golf hustler's red Ford Taurus.

HOMESTEAD FARMS GOLF RESORT

115 E Homestead Boulevard, Lynden, WA 98264
800-354-1196 • www.homesteadfarmsgolf.com
Architect/Year: Bill Overdorf, 1993
Tees/Yardages: 4 sets of tees from 5,570 to 7,001 yards
Season: Year-round
Cost: $$ to $$$
Tee times: Up to 1 week in advance

LAKE PADDEN MUNICIPAL GOLF COURSE

4882 S Amish Way, Bellingham, WA 98229
360-738-7400 • www.lakepadden.com
Architects/Year: Roy Goss and Glen Proctor, 1972
Tees/Yardages: 3 sets of tees from 5,484 to 6,575 yards
Season: Year-round
Cost: $ to $$
Tee times: Up to 1 week in advance

SEMIAHMOO RESORT

8720 Semiahmoo Parkway, Blaine, WA 98230
800-231-4425 • www.semiahmoo.com

Semiahmoo Golf and Country Club

Architect/Year: Arnold Palmer, 1987
Tees/Yardages: 4 sets of tees from 5,288 to 7,005 yards
Season: Year-round
Cost: $$ to $$$
Tee times: Up to 30 days in advance

Loomis Trail Golf and Country Club

Architect/Year: Graham Cooke, 1993
Tees/Yardages: 4 sets of tees from 5,399 to 7,137 yards
Season: Year-round
Cost: $$ to $$$
Tee times: Up to 30 days in advance

SHUKSAN GOLF CLUB

1500 E Axton Road, Bellingham, WA 98226
800-801-8897 • www.shuksangolf.com
Architect/Year: Rick Dvorak, 1994
Tees/Yardages: 3 sets of tees from 5,271 to 6,742 yards
Season: Year-round
Cost: $ to $$
Tee times: Up to 2 weeks in advance, locals up to 1 week in advance

SUDDEN VALLEY GOLF AND COUNTRY CLUB

4 Clubhouse Circle, Bellingham, WA 98229
360-734-6435 • www.suddenvalleygolf.com
Architect/Year: Ted Robinson, 1970
Tees/Yardages: 4 sets of tees from 5,627 to 6,553 yards
Season: Year-round
Cost: $ to $$
Tee times: Up to 1 week in advance

COLUMBIA RIVER

A FORTY-FIVE-MINUTE scenic drive east of Portland, **DOLCE SKAMANIA LODGE** exudes the natural beauty of the rugged Northwest. Skamania is a lovely, laid-back property and its golf course, while a bit short and narrow, is pure fun.

Just inside the heavy-timber construction and board-and-batten siding of Skamania's Cascadian-style exterior, the three-story Gorge Room welcomes visitors with floor-to-ceiling windows overlooking wildflower meadows and the Columbia River. Arts and Crafts furnishings cluster around a stone hearth blazing with sweet-scented logs. The two-hundred-year-old wood flooring is laid with thick Native American rugs. Paintings, petroglyph rubbings, and other works from artists throughout the Pacific

◀ *Desert Canyon: Orondo, Washington*

Northwest adorn the walls. Guests at Skamania Lodge actually gather in the Gorge Room, and in the upstairs library's thick leather chairs, to read, sip cocktails, and tell interminable stories about their third shots on the difficult sixteenth hole.

The lodge's guest rooms are also decorated in the rich, woodsy mountain lodge tradition of national parks. Other facilities include a fitness center with an indoor swimming pool, outdoor tennis courts, spa treatment rooms, and an outdoor whirlpool in a natural rock setting. The views at Skamania are epic, and the very best one is of distant mountain peaks and morning mists swirling down the gorge, as seen from the steaming waters of the whirlpool before a breakfast of salmon hash in the Cascade Room. Skamania's restaurant serves up the freshest and finest of the region—from local oysters to trout, salmon, and tender game. The wood-burning oven turns out some particularly memorable specialty breads and roasted meats.

Each hole of the Dolce Skamania Lodge's golf course was sculpted from forests of Douglas fir, red cedar, maple, and ash. Many tees offer views of river and mountains, but virtually no holes look onto other holes—or upon other golfers struggling along in the rough—thereby lending the course an insular feel. Several hiking loops wrap around the course, crossing creeks, passing lakes, winding through woodlands and wetlands, descending canyons, skirting wildflower meadows, and offering views of the Columbia River, forested mountains, and the occasional awkward golfer shanking an iron shot into the trees.

This par-70 layout may seem easy to skilled players because of its short length (5,836 yards from the back tees), but golfers with a bit less control may feel as if they've been out hiking in the woods. In fact, some locals joke that the fairways are so narrow that foursomes must walk them in single file. A local rule allows you to treat the woods as a lateral hazard, which helps speed up play. The course was designed by Northwest golf course architect Gene "Bunny" Mason, whose signature is to place trees in the middle of fairways—often where trees just don't belong. While on a good day many golfers will eat this course for lunch, on a bad day you might become local cuisine.

Skamania is the Chinook Indian word for "swift water," which is especially appropriate because more than seventy waterfalls plunge within visiting distance of the lodge. When you're tired of golfing, or you've lost all your golf balls, hike, mountain bike, tour wineries, raft, ski (even in summer), or visit ice caves, lava beds, and dams. Skamania Lodge is now the catch phrase for a destination resort that integrates activities and relaxation, and where travelers can balance all the elements that make for a great golf getaway.

101

While Washington State is deservedly known for many enticing characteristics, it hasn't exactly developed a reputation for fine desert golf. "But avast!" you might say if you've visited the **DESERT CANYON GOLF RESORT** in Orondo, way up the Columbia River from Skamania Lodge, on the east side of the Cascades, three hours from both Seattle and Spokane.

Located in a high desert valley full of sagebrush and fruit orchards, Desert Canyon offers Southwestern-style desert golf without the shops full of kachina dolls and dusty chile peppers, though you can probably still find a Corona or a Dos Equis in the bar. The property offers a variety of accommodation types and is associated with the Great Links Golf Resorts.

The golf here is as big as the landscape itself, luxuriating deeply and greenly against the surrounding dun-colored mountains full of rattlesnakes. The aptly named **LAKES** and **DESERT** nines play ubiquitously up- or downhill amid, well, lakes and desert. Most holes flirt with water or canyon crossings.

The **LAKES** side opens with a sweeping downhill par 4 of 401 yards with a green nearly squeezed in two by water. The second hole introduces a less-than-congenial waste bunker that you need to carry off the tee. Number three presents a long uphill par 5 of 542; avoid a grassy depression that crosses the fairway 250 yards from the green. Number six is a particularly good hole—391 yards on which you must carry a hilltop for a view of the putting surface. The fairway bends right, and a bunker will punish power fades on the approach. Number seven plays 576 yards worth staying left on off the tee; trees and a bunker right present danger. Your second shot should roll up to the very edge of a canyon 217 yards out from the farther of two greens (the shorter one is for players using the two forward sets of tees). Number eight on the Lakes side is a 226-yard downhill par 3 with a three-tiered green showing off a shapely hourglass figure. The hole crosses a waste area and presents views of high, arid hills beyond the green.

The **DESERT** side begins with a reachable par 5 of 539 yards—it's worth noting that this is the shortest of the long holes. Number two plays a mere 338 yards, but a canyon accompanies you along the right side the entire way before darting in front of a two-tiered target. Better save some mojo for number six, Desert Canyon's big signature hole. Enjoy the views from the elevated tees of this 679-yard behemoth. Scout the horizon for the lone pine beside the green and a flag rippling in the breeze like the sail of a distant ship on the horizon. Either you'll feel as far away as a marooned sailor or you'll get that sensation created by the carnival ride where the floor drops out from under you. Maybe both. Staying left on your second shot will shorten the journey here, but hitting right toward a directional bunker represents a safer strategy. You'll be happy to reach this green whenever it happens. Catch your breath on the 135-yard seventh hole and remember that cacti, while attractive, prefer not to be hugged. Overall, Desert Canyon is tough and memorable all the way around, with plenty of forced carries over gaping ravines, waste areas, and other assorted horrors. It is in mint condition, and a delight to play.

The eighteen-hole championship putting course will delight as well. It's best enjoyed around 1:00 A.M., following a couple of the aforementioned Coronas or Dos Equis. The par-72 course is a marvel—smooth as a buzz cut and full of undulations, sand traps, water hazards, and giant breaks—and really, really fun.

Dolce Skamania:
Stevenson, Washington ▶

DESERT CANYON GOLF RESORT

1201 Desert Canyon Boulevard, Orondo, WA 98843
800-258-4173 • www.desertcanyon.com
Architect/Year: Jack Frei, 1993
Tees/Yardages: 5 sets of tees from 4,939 to 7,217 yards
Season: March to October
Cost: $$ to $$$$
Tee times: No restrictions with credit card, otherwise up to 1 week in advance

DOLCE SKAMANIA LODGE

1131 Skamania Lodge Way, Stevenson, WA 98648
800-293-0418
www.dolce.com/skamania/dolce_skamania.html
Architect/Year: Gene "Bunny" Mason, 1993
Tees/Yardages: 3 sets of tees from 4,362 to 5,836 yards
Season: Year-round
Cost: $ to $$$
Tee times: Lodge guests no restrictions, nonguests up to 1 week in advance

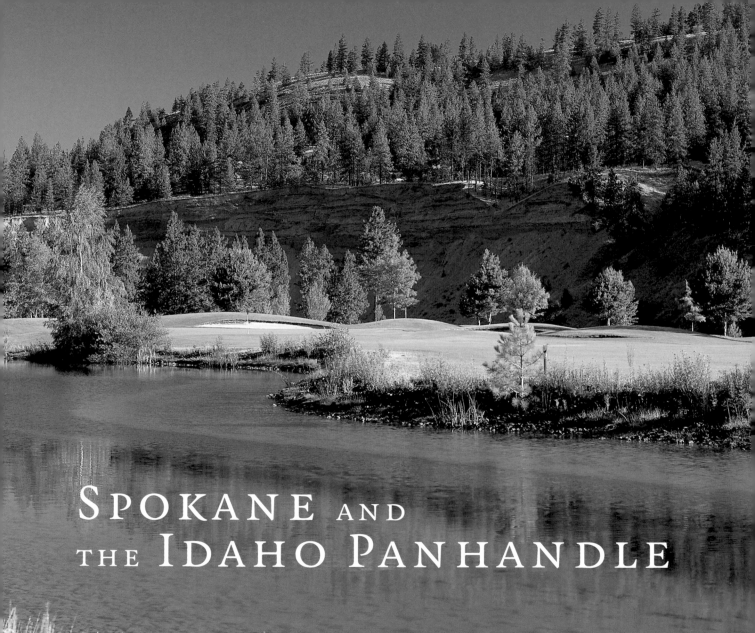

SPOKANE AND THE IDAHO PANHANDLE

OKAY, QUICK—name the second-largest city in Washington state. For that matter, name *any* city in Washington other than Seattle. Bonus points will be awarded for correctly pronouncing Spokane (spo-CAN), one of the most fetching small urban areas in the American West. In recent years various national magazines have touted Spokane as one of the nation's top outdoor towns, one of the best places to raise a family, and among the top twenty-five U.S. cities for small businesses.

This unspoiled outpost of 188,000 (400,000 including the surrounding metro area) radiates from a downtown clustered along the dramatic Spokane River, whose massive falls crash beside 100-acre

◄ *The Creek at Qualchan: Spokane, Washington*

Spread through four distinct seasons, 260 days of sunshine beam
down upon historical western architecture and inviting cityscapes
bursting with gardens and public art.

Recent investment has resulted in such distinctive historic renovations as the boutiquey Kempis Hotel—an all-suites hostelry adorned
with antiques, hand-painted murals of Italian garden scenes, and a
three-story atrium gurgling with a flower-filled fountain. Similar
efforts turned a 1916 steam plant into a retail and office complex
where visitors can dine in former boilers at the Steam Plant Grill, visit
what was once the coal bunker, and ogle the piping, columns, beams,
skylights, and other oddities from this Kirtland Cutter architectural
classic. Be sure to work up enough steam to down a Centennial Pale
Ale or Polar Bear Stout from the Coeur D'Alene Brewery on-site. Other
recent renovations in town include the lovingly restored Davenport
Hotel and the newly expanded Museum of Arts and Culture. The $30
million surgery was designed to convert the museum into a trophy
spouse anchoring the new Davenport Arts District.

On the first Sunday in May, Spokane hosts Bloomsday, the world's
largest timed foot race. At the end of June, 110,000 participants drib-
ble and pass through town for Hoopfest, the largest three-on-three
basketball tournament in the world. The surrounding country is full

of lakes, streams, trails, and bike paths and close to some equally wonderful places just across the border into Idaho. I won't even ask you to name a city in Idaho.

What could possibly make such a desirable small-town metropolis even more attractive? How about eighteen golf courses within an hour's drive? These layouts range from downbeat munis to one of the most revered resorts in the United States; what they have in common is an ambiance that's been lost in much of America. They're the kinds of courses where the pro has remained for more than just a year or two and has embossed some personality on the place. Locals play in jeans and drink domestic beer straight from the can in the grill room alongside the maintenance crew, and while residents worry about increased green fees, outsiders will have two words for them: Hello-o! Where else can travelers play such solid venues for around $20, or can locals buy a multiplay card and steal golf rounds for little more than half that much?

A number of courses in the Spokane area are managed by city or county recreation departments—good news because this ensures friendly, well-managed golf at unbelievable rates. One of the muni crown jewels is the **INDIAN CANYON GOLF COURSE**, an old Chandler Egan track built in 1935. Head pro Gary Lindeblad has been Indian

Canyon's chief for seventeen years and owes no corporate allegiances. This is golf like it used to be.

The richly turfed course was good enough to twice host the USGA Men's Public Links Championship (in 1941 and 1984). Egan's routing plays 6,255 yards from the warrior tees and encompasses sensible par 3s ranging from 121 to 224 yards, narrow fairways, hidden hazards, and crowned greens. Most holes are especially playful close to the pin. As on other Egan tracks, the difficulty is subtle; while the course looks easy on paper, paper is generally flat—a condition that won't characterize many lies here. Further, Lindeblad takes pride in "letting the rough grow up until everyone complains." One local stick recently inquired whether the pro's mower had broken down.

Indian Canyon opens well with two short par 5s, the first playing downhill, the second featuring an amphitheater green that kicks balls toward a greenside bunker you can't see from the fairway. Number six, a short par 4, presents a rare opportunity to land on level ground. Hole seven offers big guys a chance to fire at the green 287 yards away, but most should hit 215 to the knee of the sharp dogleg. In the 1940s, Ben Hogan called the 224-yard eighth the toughest single-shot hole he'd ever seen.

The back nine begins with another downhill romp from a box that

Indian Canyon:
Spokane, Washington ▶

tees up views of downtown Spokane and a gaggle of mountains. Added height provides balls with plenty of time to decide whether to hook or slice. Number fourteen weighs in as one of the state's toughest holes: 438 yards through a narrow canyon. Risk a little reward on the 267-yard seventeenth, with a double-tiered green. Lindeblad suggests that being even a little right here magically transforms a three into a seven.

South of downtown Spokane, Bob Baldock hung his signature on the **HANGMAN VALLEY GOLF COURSE** in 1965. The 6,906-yard track tightens the noose with plenty of challenge across open, high-desert-like river valley terrain.

Hangman begins with a narrow fairway that kicks balls hard right to a blind landing area—assuming you hit past the forward tees. A ubiquitously musical creek tinkles past beyond the green, introducing a recurring theme. Number two allows for some breath catching with a wide fairway that luxuriates between bunkers right and the creek meandering left. The tiny green is framed by more bunkers and a charming willow. The front side ends par 3, par 5, par 3.

The flip side opens with a solid par 5 demanding a creek carry, followed by a very good par 3 of 193 yards with a lake and waterfall protecting the left side. At this point you'll have played five holes in a row without a par 4. You may also have noticed that nearly every green is framed by two bunkers—a design element that grows somewhat tiresome. The back side is also largely routed along the dreaded up-and-back theme. All in all, though, Hangman ropes you in with its charms—especially when played in the company of home pro Steve Nelke.

Farther along the same stream that lends watery character to Hangman Valley, and with similar drops and rises in elevation as at Indian Canyon, lies **THE CREEK AT QUALCHAN**, a 1993 Bill Robinson design. The 6,599-yard venue exudes a more familiar modern feel and emphasizes thinking and placement across its sprawling footprint. The high drama begins on the first tee, which orbits way above a fairway that can be reached with the most style points by flying over several tall pines and a couple of bunkers. Number three presents a buff 537-yard par 5 where you must launch a field goal between ponderosa uprights, but beware of attaining the left bunker. The frontal closing hole is a handsome 338 yards across a creek where a big hill deflects drives to the left, allowing you to pretend you hit a draw.

The back nine begins sharply with a dogleg right that some might consider going for even at 379 yards. Two bunkers tighten the landing area; another lurks like Ralph Nader—a little left of the green.

Head pro Mark Gardner calls number twelve Qualchan's toughest—a 450-yard par 4 with a tight fairway and challenging angles. Sixteen and eighteen cordially request carries over the creek, and eighteen is further toughened by downhill lies that will dilute your loft. The course ends par 5, par 4, par 5, suggesting that you reserve some wood mojo for late in the day.

Still in Spokane, the stately old **DOWNRIVER GOLF COURSE** lies—not surprisingly—down the river from town in a treed valley with waterside views and a sylvan, picnicky feel. The happy layout is overseen

◄ *Hangman Valley:*
Spokane, Washington

by head pro and trick-shot artist Steve Conner, who can slam a full swing off the tee with his driver and still have his ball land behind him. The par-71 6,130-yard venue opened in 1927 and was designed by a local citizens committee back in the days when citizens committees must have gotten along. While in the pro shop, be sure to look for the scrapbook from the women's event held in 1960.

Further establishing a local theme, Downriver's first hole drops precipitously to a wide, welcoming, tree-lined fairway that makes a turn to the left. The front side sneaks an extra par 3 into the mix, and the back features consecutive par 5s at thirteen and fourteen. A smooth cocktail of riverside holes and plateau holes, an occasional blind shot, and shady river views make Downriver the kind of course you'll remember. It's also worth remembering that when a bunch of holes play downhill, you'll eventually have to make up that elevation if you want to get back to your car. Not even Steve Conner can shoot his way around that law of physics.

Heading east out of Spokane toward the state of famous potatoes, it's worth stopping at the lovely MEADOWWOOD GOLF COURSE. This 1988 vintage Robert Muir Graves design plays a moderately burly 6,874. A local developer gave the county enough land to build its golf course, and he retained the surrounding lots, which he's begun developing.

The greens here are shapely and the fairway bunkers surgically placed. Rolling, moundy, open terrain encourages a good mood, as does affable head pro Bob Scott, who loves nothing more than to play in a cold rain.

Following a couple of challenging warm-up holes, number three presents the first serious dilemmas, namely what to hit off the tee and where to aim. Two invisible yin-yang bunkers guard the right side, and a long drive left will punch through the fairway and splash into the lake. Number six presents a 164-yard par 3 with bunkers circling up like wagons under attack. Wind direction plays a major role here. The front concludes with several pure holes that are like good parents: They present clear choices and obvious consequences.

The back opens semi-goofily with a 398-yard dogleg around a lake with a fairway that cants toward the water. An ideal tee shot might soar 180 to 190 yards. Long hitters will not benefit from their driving prowess unless they execute perfect shots. The par-3 seventh hole offers two lakes—one for hooks and one for slices—and a green-fronting bunker that must be airlifted. This nine ups the fun quotient by asking jocularly for well-placed drives and clever negotiation of the bunkering. Many locals consider the 607-yard lazily doglegging sixteenth one of the best holes in the area. One bunker causes havoc to the right of the first landing area, then two more gang up on the left side of the second landing. The hole plays uphill between specta-tor pines. Seventeen, a blind, uphill 165-yard par 3, will play auto-matic ball return if you come up short of the tiered green.

Just over the border into Idaho, drift on in to the **HIGHLANDS GOLF AND COUNTRY CLUB**, in Post Falls. This owner-designed course, opened in 1991, plays a very short 6,306 yards. Why is it that modern short courses never seem as satisfying as old-style short courses? This one was clearly built to support housing, as is further evidenced by the recent rerouting. Anyone who can figure out how the original layout played should win a free club-head cover.

Still, there's some fine golf at Highlands, beginning with one of the best practice areas in the Gemstone State. Cards on each bag stand indicate distances to the many flags flapping across the huge range. Well-designed stations for chipping, pitching, bunker play, and putting may have you thinking you can actually improve your game. The entire property sits atop a 250-foot bluff, providing great views, and the impressive plantings lend a manicured country-club ambiance. Other memorable touches include the strangely lovely humped bunkers—some shaped like lightning—which must be hell to mow.

Highlands begins with a 467-yard par 5 featuring a lake right of the green. If you lay up, stay short of the lone pine or your ball might slide downhill into the hazard. This hole should sound a warning. The course is short but narrow, and your shots must emulate a sixties protest song: Right on! Number six here will definitely stir debate: It plays 109 windblown yards over a slope of juniper shrubs to a green that slopes toward you. And don't go over, because the bicuspid-shaped back bunker will take a bite out of your score.

The back opens with a tight, enigmatic 608-yarder with three blind shots. Next comes a par 5 of a measly 438 yards, which is like threading a needle after bench-pressing 250 pounds. Nearly all of Highlands's length measures between holes seven and eleven: three par 5s ranging from 438 to 608 yards and a 433-yard par 4. The 408-yard home hole demands a drive between or past fairway bunkers; a good poke will squirt down the business side of a steep hill. Consider laying up on the second shot, and stay out of the five toe-shaped bunkers behind the foot pad of the green.

Surely Idaho's **COEUR D'ALENE RESORT** has executed one of the greatest marketing campaigns in golf history by making a short, really-good-but-not-great golf course into one of the most famous in the world—based largely on the uniqueness of a single hole. Although the Scott Miller design plays a mere 6,309 yards soaking wet, with a lightweight slope of 121, it's still impossible not to love this course. As easygoing head pro Mike DeLong has noticed, even guys who complain the layout is too easy leave happy over their scores and often come back. Coeur D'Alene is not a course to beat so much as one to show off on, and a day here will prove more memorable than most golf outings because of crisp service, immaculate groundskeeping, and that darned floating green. All groundskeeping is done at night to further enhance your experience, and knowledgeable forecaddies accompany every group.

Located on the site of an old lumber mill, the course is designed around four distinct geographic features: lakeshore, forested ridge, gently rolling woodlands, and Fernand Creek, a revitalized trout stream. It boasts four sets of tees and the banked fairways kick most shots back toward center; you'd be hard-pressed to find much rough, even with my game. The trees have been thinned enough to minimize their negative impact.

This grassy adventure begins with two showy long holes—a 526-yard par 5 and a 436-yard par 4, but the layout squanders most of its front-nine length right there. The next four holes play 128, 277, 108, and 167, leading you to wonder if you've accidentally stumbled onto the pitch-and-putt course—except for the absolute perfection of the terrain and the extensive plantings. Number four may present the best challenge on the front side; it's a dogleg left with a nasty bunker guarding the uphill turn. The conservative play is a 175-yard line drive to set up an approach over a rock outcropping to the small platform green. Though only 277 yards, the design makes this a two-shot hole. Call Gamblers Anonymous if you decide to go for it. Holes five and six offer back-to-back par 3s that are eligible for anyone's photo album.

Following the turn, number eleven would be one of the best holes on the course if a local rule didn't provide for a free drop out of the junipers left of the green. An angled creek makes going for glory in two from 530 yards daunting until you realize you can miss way left without penalty. Finally you'll come to the superstar fourteenth with the moveable floating green—which might be improved by requiring golfers to hit to it *while* it's moving. Even if you're as cynical as me, you can't help but enjoy the heck out of this experience, including the boat ride to the drop area, er, I mean green. During my visit, my friend John bounced his tee shot off the wooden boat landing beside the green, leading his caddie to remark ruefully, "I don't think the dock is holding today."

The Coeur D'Alene Resort is way more than just one unforgettable golf hole and one good golf course—it's an anomaly in this land of chain motels and small, rustic lodges. The signature restaurant has won awards for its wine list, the spa offers an ample menu of treatments, and guests can raft, fish, bike, ride horseback, or relax in spacious rooms with decks that feel like high diving boards perched above the very beautiful blue lake.

Nearby to the Coeur D'Alene Resort, the new **CIRCLING RAVEN GOLF CLUB**—part of the Coeur D'Alene Casino Resort—opened for play late in 2003. The 7,189-yard Gene Bates design routes through forested meadows and wetlands and offers more excitement than a pot-stakes Texas Hold 'Em hand.

For an interesting golf juxtaposition, travel forty-three miles north from Coeur D'Alene to **HIDDEN LAKES GOLF RESORT**, in Sandpoint, ranked as one of the toughest layouts in Idaho. This vacation town beside Lake Pend Oreille is home to seventy-five hundred folks and the well-loved Coldwater Creek Company, which sells clothing and gift items through catalogs and at a unique retail space on the Cedar Street Bridge, modeled after Florence's Ponte Vecchio.

Local architect Jim Krause designed Hidden Lakes's original layout, which opened in 1986. Hatch Mueller substituted a few new holes that debuted to deserved acclaim. The recently added stone and timber clubhouse is also stunningly impressive. The owners have done everything right here—including insisting that moose are still always allowed to play through.

The back tees stretch to 6,923 yards with a 136 slope, but the blues proffer a manageable 6,084 yards. Both sets provide great views of the Selkirk Mountains. The Pack River makes many cameo appearances; in fact, the course might be more aptly named Hidden River. Golfers must carry water on seven holes and avoid it in one form or another on all but three. Mueller's new holes are built on an island, which should tell you something about the availability of H_2O. Fortunately for me, a fade comes in handy here as most of the trouble has been engineered on the left. Greens slope but don't really tier or undulate.

Things start out cordially as your first drive splits two big aspens before the hole turns left. The ninth here is a truly great hole, dogging right around a giant snag, with the river flowing by on your right. Hit 180 off the tee and carry water (and chop wood) on your second shot on this 404-yarder. Ten is one of Hidden Lakes's new holes, and presents narrow openings between bunkers on both sides of a fairway that slopes toward the water. The green is circled by birches, and the bunker is full of moose prints. The middle of the back nine features some nice but slightly farmlandish holes located amid real estate. When I mentioned this to wacky master pro Ken Parker, he said that, speaking of real estate, I must have seen a lot of it on number fifteen. Finish this round with another big river crossing on the eighteenth and you'll feel a little like Mark Twain negotiating the Mississippi.

If Hidden Lakes proves a little much for you, why not detour to nearby Hayden Lake, home of Henry-Griffitts, precision fitting and golf club manufacturers—the first guys to really custom-fit clubs. Current resident gurus Ross and Randy Henry (cofounder Jim Griffitts is deceased) have kept their fine company small (they make seventy-thousand clubs annually, compared to seventy million made by the big guys) to ensure quality. Their irons, especially, are as good as any you'll find, and the company stands behind its equipment and its customers. Also, Ross Henry possesses an uncanny knack for making birdies out of fairway bunkers.

Given all the wonders and attractions of the inland Northwest—including more than a half-dozen super golf venues (most at ludicrously low prices)—you'll no doubt wonder why the area is still virtually unknown in much of the country. Please—keep your voice down and your questions to yourself!

SPOKANE AND THE IDAHO PANHANDLE: *Courses*

CIRCLING RAVEN GOLF CLUB

27068 S Highway 95, Coeur D'Alene, ID 83876
800-523-2464 • www.cdacasino.com
Architect/Year: Gene Bates, 2003
Tees/Yardages: 5 sets of tees from 4,708 to 7,189 yards
Season: April to October
Cost: $$$
Tee times: No restrictions

COEUR D'ALENE RESORT

900 Floating Green Drive, Coeur D'Alene, ID 83815
800-688-5253 • www.cdaresort.com
Architect/Year: Scott Miller, 1991
Tees/Yardages: 5 sets of tees from 4,448 to 6,751 yards
Season: April to October
Cost: $$$$$
Tee times: Resort guests no restrictions, nonguests up to 30 days in advance

THE CREEK AT QUALCHAN

301 E Meadowlane Road, Spokane, WA 99224
509-448-9317 • www.spokaneparks.org/golf
Architect/Year: Bill Robinson, 1993
Tees/Yardages: 3 sets of tees from 5,538 to 6,599 yards
Season: March to November
Cost: $
Tee times: Up to 1 week in advance for weekends, 1 day in advance for weekdays

DOWNRIVER GOLF COURSE

3225 N Columbia Circle, Spokane, WA 99205
509-327-5269
Architect/Year: Local Citizens Committee, 1916
Tees/Yardages: 3 sets of tees from 5,592 to 6,130 yards
Season: March to November
Cost: $
Tee times: Up to 1 week in advance for weekends, 1 day in advance for weekdays; no restrictions for nonresidents reserving with credit card

HIDDEN LAKES GOLF RESORT

151 Clubhouse Way, Sandpoint, ID 83864
888-806-6673 • www.hiddenlakesgolf.com
Architect/Year: Jim Krause, 1986
Tees/Yardages: 4 sets of tees from 5,157 to 6,923 yards
Season: April to November
Cost: $$$, including cart
Tee times: Up to 1 year in advance with credit card

HANGMAN VALLEY GOLF COURSE

2210 E Hangman Valley Road, Spokane, WA 99223
509-448-1212
Architects/Year: Bob Baldock and Sons, 1969
Tees/Yardages: 3 sets of tees from 5,699 to 6,906 yards
Season: March to October
Cost: $
Tee times: Up to 1 week in advance

HIGHLANDS GOLF AND COUNTRY CLUB

5500 E Mullan Avenue, Post Falls, ID 83854
888-900-3673
Architect/Year: Jim Kraus, 1990
Tees/Yardages: 3 sets of tees from 5,125 to 6,506 yards
Season: March to November
Cost: $
Tee times: Up to 1 week in advance for weekends, 1 day in advance for weekdays

INDIAN CANYON GOLF COURSE

4304 West Drive, Spokane, WA 99224
509-747-5353 • www.spokaneparks.com
Architect/Year: Chandler Egan, 1935
Tees/Yardages: 3 sets of tees from 5,336 to 6,285 yards
Season: April to October
Cost: $
Tee times: No restrictions

MEADOWWOOD GOLF COURSE

24501 E Valleyway Avenue, Liberty Lake, WA 99019
509-255-9539 • www.meadowwoodgolf.com
Architect/Year: Robert Muir Graves, 1988
Tees/Yardages: 3 sets of tees from 5,880 to 6,874 yards
Season: March to November
Cost: $
Tee times: No restrictions for nonresidents

SUN VALLEY AND MCCALL

IN 1936, Union Pacific railroad magnate Averell Harriman sent a scout out west to discover the best location in America for a new ski resort. The scout chose Sun Valley, Idaho, where the first chairlift, based on a banana hoist, dragged bunches of skiers up the lovely mountains. The current Sun Valley Resort—including the lodge and inn—is a four-season golf and ski destination with literally hundreds of guestrooms from which to choose. It's also the rare place where you can return from a round of golf to go ice-skating year-round on a beautiful rink out back. If falling down on a frozen surface is not your idea of fun, watch other people doing it from beside the fireplace in the oak-paneled living room upstairs. The lodge in particular exudes European

◀ Sun Valley Resort: Sun Valley, Idaho

127

style in a Rocky Mountain setting. Its handmade wildflower carpets softened the steps of such notables as Gary Cooper, Clark Gable, and Marilyn Monroe. Nineteen films were shot on location here and Hemingway worked on *For Whom the Bell Tolls* on the second floor, nearly calling it For Whom the Dinner Bell Tolls.

It tolls for thee. Get yourself to the Lodge Dining Room, a formal, Old World restaurant where music tinkles as delicately as the crystal. Order the braised stew of rabbit and fennel with red wine and puff pastry fleurons—and not just because it's fun to say "fleurons." The dining room offers comforting classical continental cuisine. Or try Gretchen's for quesadillas, burgers, and the like. And you will like.

You'll also like the Robert Trent Jones Jr.–designed, high mountain/ desert golf course, which stretches to 6,846 yards and has been ranked as the best layout in Idaho. Holes on the SUN VALLEY RESORT GOLF COURSE wind between some of the gentlest, most sculpted, and curvaceous mountains you've ever seen. The course changes demeanor suddenly. After a welcoming 363-yard par-4 opener, number two shocks with another par 4 that's more than 80 yards longer. Oh yeah, and it doglegs left and makes two stream crossings. Rest up a bit on the 120-yard fifth before holes seven through eleven show off further liquid assets. On the twelfth, a calm par 4, watch out for

Rocky and Bullwinkle—two bunkers fronting the green.

The course ends with two par 3s in the last four holes—but the first of these is 244 yards. As you face the eighteenth you'll feel like another Hemingway title—"The Old Man on the Tee."

Located in the intermountain west—100 miles north of Boise, Idaho, on the shores of Payette Lake—lies what may be the best woodsy, mountain golf retreat ever designed in the style of Aspen and Jackson Hole. **THE WHITETAIL CLUB** is a sort of rich, elegant cousin to great Rocky Mountain golf destinations. Combining rugged western flavor with elegant European accents, Whitetail stands as a sporting lodge in the grandest tradition.

The seventy-seven guest rooms—most with stunning lake views—and welcoming public rooms are a veritable United Nations of influences: European tapestries, German-carved mahogany furniture, Italian linens, cut crystal from Austria, and cathedral-size bathrooms and bedrooms. The lodge features hand-hewn log construction and the plushest sofas, a game room, a movie theater, and other amenities. Upon opening in 2002, Whitetail joined the ranks of the most luxurious private club/resorts anywhere in the United States.

Andy North and Roger Packard designed the 7,012-yard golf course that routes through pines, meadows, and wildflowers, between trout ponds and giant boulders, in the shadows of the Jug Handle and Council Mountains. Native grasses and alpine breezes lend a mountain freshness. You must be a resort guest to play the course.

Whitetail begins with a 390-yard dogleg right that drops down to a bowl fronted on the right by a bunker and several of the signature boulders that lend the course a clean, natural feel. Overall, Whitetail offers a small collection of generous doglegs that favor slicers. Two of the first four holes here are par 5s (510 and 478 yards). The eighth hole offers the kind of risk/reward par 4 that every golf course should have: 310 right-doglegging yards where you can attack the green with a power fade or a long ball that carries over trees.

The back side continues the visual treats. Number eleven may be one of the best on the course—374 yards of tight downhill dogleg left. Catch a ridge along the left side, and you'll hitch a free ride to the bottom in front of an elevated green. Shorter tee shots may leave testy downhill lies. The final holes break out into the open amid lakes and stone bridges and rocky streams.

Whitetail's golf course is as ruggedly handsome as the lodge is buttery fine.

Whitetail: McCall, Idaho ▶

SUN VALLEY RESORT

1 Sun Valley Road, Sun Valley, ID 83353
800-786-8259 • www.sunvalley.com
Architect/Year: Robert Trent Jones Jr., 1980
Tees/Yardages: 3 to 4 sets of tees from 5,380 to 6,892 yards
Season: April to October
Cost: $$ to $$$$$
Tee times: Resort guests no restrictions nonguests up to 2 weeks in advance

WHITETAIL CLUB

501 W Lake Street, McCall, ID 83638
800-657-6464 • www.whitetailclub.com
Architects/Year: Andy North and Roger Packard, 2002
Season: Memorial Day to September
Cost: $$$$$
Tee times: Lodge guests only, up to 30 days in advance

FLATHEAD VALLEY

JUST AS THE BEST RESTAURANTS often pair each course of a fine dinner with a wine that complements its subtle flavors, the best golf destinations offer the possibility of pairing a great course with some full-bodied activity that complements a morning of swinging your clubs. In Montana's Flathead Valley, golf pairs well with such vintage sports as hiking, rafting, biking, fishing, and more golf. Within thirty miles of the resort enclave of Whitefish, and a mere moraine's length from Glacier National Park, lie nine golf courses and an extensive menu of accompanying outdoor pursuits, not to mention a healthy population of grizzly bears. With luck the term "grizzly" won't apply to your game.

◀ *Mission Mountain Country Club: Ronan, Montana*

133

Located at the base of the Big Mountain Resort, Whitefish itself is home to the **WHITEFISH LAKE GOLF CLUB**, the only thirty-six-hole complex in the Big Sky State. The **NORTH COURSE** was built by loggers working for the WPA back in the 1930s, which explains the hand-hewn lodgepole pine clubhouse. When this layout initially ran into financial trouble, management offered twenty-five-cent memberships to help finish construction and hire a pro. A second nine was added in the 1950s. This charming classic plays 6,579 yards from the back tees. Three cuts of grabby rough and bunkers that are more decorative than penal join with lake, mountain, and forest views. A number of blind shots over and around hills will help to keep you alert as you gulp down the scenery. The back nine is especially lubricious as the course winds its way toward Flathead Lake.

And might I suggest a walk in the treetops to fill out your day of golf? Guides from the Big Mountain Resort will lead you on this high-level adventure sixty feet above the forest floor. Begin with a taste of mountain biking on the mile-long ride from the resort to an authentic cowboy line camp. On the day of my visit, fresh grizzly claw marks decorated a post here, reminding me that in case of an attack I needn't outrun the bear, only the people accompanying me. After a safety orientation and gear familiarization, I followed my guide way up into the canopy of Douglas fir, pine, cedar, and tama-rack. Safely belayed to fixed cables, we strolled along narrow planks swinging in the breeze.

The Grouse Mountain Lodge—a wonder of wood, glass, and stone—overlooks Whitefish Lake's **SOUTH COURSE** and has a sun porch perfect for sipping morning coffee and watching the antics of golfers. If you don't have much of a game on the links, have some game (read: venison or buffalo) for dinner at the lodge's Logan's Grill. Then lay back by the lobby's three-story river rock fireplace and catch a snooze. Better yet, get a room—some of which have lofts and private Jacuzzis.

Eagle Bend: Bigfork, Montana ▶

In the morning, check out the South Course. Designed in 1980 by John Steidel, South encompasses wetlands, waterfowl, and narrow alder corridors stretching across 6,551 delectable yards. The large, sweepy, crowned greens lend huge breaks. Some of the best holes come in the middle of the front side. Number six, a 470-yarder, presents 241 yards to a water crossing, then cuts left. A slope fronting the green kicks balls toward a lake lined with the ghostly trunks of dead pines. Number eight's 198 yards cut across a corner of the water. The ninth tee is situated practically in the lake.

A mountain bike ride up around Big Mountain proves a fine companion to the morning's golf—just don't attempt it with Walt Chauner, director of marketing at nearby BIG MOUNTAIN GOLF COURSE. For Chauner, who tried to kill me on a ride following a round of golf together, thousand-foot climbs are as simple as knocking 280-yard drives. You can choose from among twenty miles of single track on Big Mountain, ride the eight intermediate miles of the Summit Trail, or practice stunts and obstacles (and face plants) in the Outpost Skills Park. Or opt for the fruity, easygoing Tenderfoot Trail and you'll enjoy the biking equivalent of a sweet sauterne.

Twelve miles south of Whitefish, Andy North and Roger Packard's Big Mountain Golf Course sports Bentgrass greens and wheat grass

◀ *Buffalo Hill Golf Course:*
Kalispell, Montana

137

rough (it sounds like a health drink), not to mention the aforementioned Walt Chauner. You'll want to be in good health to negotiate twenty grass bunkers, forty sand bunkers, and four holes that caper along the Stillwater River on this 7,015-yard venue. The front side is moundy and treeless—a sort of Montanan links. The more traditional back plays through woods with elevation changes. Gaze up from the deep rough at the Swan Mountains and the peaks of Glacier Park.

Many of the unique greens at Northern Pines are camouflaged by swales that only expose tiny slivers of the putting surface, thus demanding confident approaches. The course encompasses 150,000 square feet of greens but another 250,000 in tee boxes. The best hole may be number twelve, a sweeping downhill par 4 with bunkers mining the middle of the fairway. Course codesigner Andy North once commented that if he had to par in from number fourteen here to win the U.S. Open, he'd have a tough time.

Following a walk around Northern Pines, why not avoid a bike ride with the director of marketing and instead head up into Glacier National Park in the afternoon? The park encompasses 730 miles of trails in conjunction with Canada's Waterton Lakes National Park. What could be more thirst-quenching than driving just a little fast on Going-to-the-Sun Road, which sweeps through the mountains here?

This paved two-lane byway stretches fifty-two miles past high lakes and steep cliffs, proffers views of peaks and glaciers, and crosses the Continental Divide at 6,646-foot Logan Pass. There, you can hike to the Hidden Lake overlook and then follow a trail that features one-and-a-half miles of boardwalk, a section of snow crossings, and a trail to a lake full of huge, friendly fish. Or head to refreshing Iceberg Lake at the base of three-thousand-foot cliffs. Local legend contends that the lake is home to rare, fur-bearing trout.

Close by to Glacier Park in the town of Columbia Falls lies **MEADOW LAKE GOLF RESORT**. The 6,718-yard Dick Phelps design offers well-cared-for, country-club-style golf. The front side of this solid

Big Mountain Golf Club: Kalispell, Montana ▶

139

collection of holes includes such standouts as the 183-yard third, which plays over a grassy meadow. On the back side, number fifteen sips well—this straightaway 449-yarder has a tree in the middle of the fairway before the green. The finishing hole is short at 339 yards, but the crafty design calls for a layup off the tee to the brink of a water hazard followed by a laser wedge to the green.

Play Meadow Lake in the morning so that you can enjoy a rafting trip along the bubbly, sparkling Flathead River in the afternoon. Wild River Adventures offers everything from half-day tastings to entire cases (as long as six days) of whitewater fun. Consider piloting one of

the outfitter's inflatable kayaks through such rapids as Jaws or Pinball or a rapid that should look familiar to slicers: Screaming Right Turn.

Way downriver you'll find yourself close to the **BUFFALO HILL GOLF CLUB** in Kalispell—one of the most amusingly fun golf courses I've ever had the pleasure to play. John and Bill Robinson

◀ *Meadow Lake Resort: Columbia Falls, Montana*

contributed the nine-hole **CAMERON COURSE** here, but the real delight is the 6,584-yard Robert Muir Graves designed **CHAMPIONSHIP COURSE**. If surprise is a virtue, Graves's wacky yet sublime layout is ready for beatification. Every hole will have you shaking your head at the strategy or just plain beauty of this up-and-down routing lovingly entwined with the Stillwater River.

Start with a blind downhill dogleg followed by a hole that climbs and dips three times along its 598 yards. Other holes call for tee shots through 100-yard chutes of trees hit from platforms perched above the river, which itself reappears in different forms throughout the day: placid, bubbly, roaring, and such. The new greens, built in 1998, slope and slant rather than undulating.

Following the rollicking adventure of Buffalo Hill, consider a calm afternoon down on Flathead Lake in Bigfork, home of tomorrow's golf odyssey. The Marina Cay Resort, located where the Swan River feeds into the largest freshwater lake in the West, is an ideal spot for boating and fishing. The town of Bigfork has also been ranked as one of the one hundred best small art towns in the United States.

Upon waking in Bigfork, you'll be close to the **EAGLE BEND GOLF CLUB**, which boasts three nines originally named after natural phenomena: Lake, Ridge, and Nicklaus. The Nicklaus holes were

141

bottled by Jack's son, who touched up nine holes originally laid out by William Hull, who is credited with the other holes, as well. The current Nicklaus/Ridge **CHAMPIONSHIP** course (of which the junior Nicklaus designed two, three, and ten through sixteen) plays to 6,724 yards. Lon Hinkle was once the pro at this venue that's been ranked best in state. Natural rock outcroppings and distant views of mountains and pine hills are just a few of the attractions.

The first few holes play in a low bowl with views of the lake. Number five features steep cliffs along the left side of a short par 3. The pro here described the well-used drop area at the sixteenth hole by saying, "It looks like Vietnam." Eagle Bend was home to a USGA Amateur Publinks Championship.

How about pairing your round at Eagle Bend with a rambling walk across the **MISSION MOUNTAIN COUNTRY CLUB** in nearby Ronan, fourteen miles south of Flathead Lake? The light and playful venue delivers some of the state's largest greens and most easygoing holes. Gary Roger Baird laid out the 6,479-yard course in an old potato field. If potatoes had eyes, they could have looked up at mountain and glacier views. Mission Mountain is the kind of place where all the golfers know each other, and they play in jeans and rancher hats. I was joined during my round by a farmer, a teacher, and a doctor.

When I remarked upon the prevalence of such local talent, one companion said, "There's a lot of local but not very much talent."

The flat course provides a fine walk across such holes as the 331-yard fifth, where you must hit 220 to cross a pond but still land short of a creek. Number ten offers a great blind dogleg left down a hill and over a marsh. Seven holes border lakes and streams.

Drink deeply of the Flathead Valley and drive carefully under its intoxicating influence.

BUFFALO HILL GOLF CLUB

1176 N Main Street, Kalispell, MT 59901
888-342-6319 • www.golfbuffalohill.com

Championship

Architect/Year: Robert Muir Graves, 1976
Tees/Yardages: 3 sets of tees from 5,223 to 6,584 yards
Season: April to October
Cost: $$
Tee times: Up to 3 days in advance

Cameron Course (nine holes)

Architects/Year: John and Bill Robinson, 1936
Tees/Yardages: 2 sets of tees from 2,950 to 3,001 yards
Season: April to October
Cost: $
Tee Times: No advance tee times

EAGLE BEND GOLF CLUB

279 Eagle Bend Drive, Bigfork, MT 59911
800-255-5674 • www.golfmt.com

Championship

Architect/Year: William Hull Jr., 1985
Tees/Yardages: 3 sets of tees from 5,397 to 6,724 yards
Season: March to November
Cost: $$ to $$$
Tee times: No restrictions

Lake (nine holes)

Architect/Year: Nicklaus Design, 1995
Tees/Yardages: 3 sets of tees from 2,559 to 3,445 yards
Season: March to November
Cost: $$ to $$$
Tee times: No restrictions

MEADOW LAKE GOLF RESORT

490 St. Andrews Drive, Columbia Falls, MT 59912
406-892-2111 • www.meadowlakegolf.com
Architect/Year: Dick Phelps, 1984
Tees/Yardages: 4 sets of tees from 5,303 to 6,718 yards
Season: April to October
Cost: $$
Tee times: No restrictions

MISSION MOUNTAIN COUNTRY CLUB

640 Stagecoach Trail, Ronan, MT 59864
406-676-4653
Architect/Year: Gary Roger Baird, 1988
Tees/Yardages: 3 sets of tees from 5,125 to 6,479 yards
Season: March to October
Cost: $
Tee times: Up to 2 days in advance

BIG MOUNTAIN GOLF CLUB

3230 Highway 93 N, Kalispell, MT 59901
800-255-5674 • www.golfmt.com
Architects/Year: Andy North and Roger Packard, 1996
Tees/Yardages: 4 sets of tees from 5,421 to 7,015 yards
Season: March to November
Cost: $$
Tee times: No restrictions

WHITEFISH LAKE GOLF CLUB

Highway 93 N, Whitefish, MT 59937
406-862-4000 • www.golfwhitefish.com

North Course

Architects/Years: WPA, 1936 and 1954; renovated by John Steidel, 1982
Tees/Yardages: 3 sets of tees from 5,556 to 6,759 yards
Season: April to October
Cost: $$
Tee times: Up to 2 days in advance

South Course

Architect/Years: John Steidel, 1980 and 1992
Tees/Yardages: 3 sets of tees from 5,361 to 6,551 yards
Season: April to October
Cost: $$
Tee times: Up to 2 days in advance

SALT LAKE CITY
AND ENVIRONS

EVER SINCE THE MORMONS headed for Utah in 1847 to escape religious persecution, the buoyant lakeside city of Salt Lake has attracted fringe elements. More recently, they've taken the form of snowboarders drawn to ten champagne ski resorts nearby and hikers and mountain bikers lured by red rock canyons a few hours south—in fact, fifteen national parks are within a day's drive of downtown. Yet many potential visitors seem to pass through Salt Lake City on their way to somewhere else. When the 2002 Winter Olympics finally enticed people to stay, many were surprised to discover a graceful, enchanting city.

Although Mormon influences are still strong here (the entire street grid emanates from Temple

◀ *Bountiful Ridge: Bountiful, Utah*

Square), you can, in fact, get a drink or a good cup of coffee—not to mention an inspired meal and a cool hotel room. Properties as varied as the huge, plush Vegas-like Grand America and the hip boutiquey Hotel Monaco (which actually created a number of "tall" rooms with overlong beds and raised sinks to attract visiting NBA players) will satisfy all types of guests. Downtown is currently abuzz with swanky eateries and brewpubs, and the fresh architecture mixes classic elements with playful designs along ultraclean extra-wide streets.

When you're ready to get out and play golf, why not start down south at the Johnny Miller–designed THANKSGIVING POINT GOLF COURSE, possibly the only golf course in the United States that's closed on

148

◄ Thanksgiving Point:
Lehi, Utah

Sundays. Financed by a Mormon family that made its money in software, the course is part of an institute, the primary purpose of which is "to provide a wholesome environment designed to educate and beautify." Which, coincidentally, is one of the primary purposes of golf. This particular course will teach you humility, among other things.

Miller's layout—home to the father/son Champions Challenge, which draws Stadlers, Nicklauses, Trevinos, and other golfing families—plays to 7,728 yards from the longest of five sets of tees. The murky Jordan River runs alongside ten holes. Three lakes and views of the sixty-acre botanical gardens (which were planned before the golf course) enhance the surroundings at an altitude of forty-five hundred feet.

Lovely and momentous bunkering defines most of these holes. A sculpted sand pit on number three stretches 100 yards along the left side of the fairway to a green that's driveable at 325 yards if you've been living a good, clean life. Of course, steroids probably wouldn't hurt. The fourth hole, a 194-yard par 3, bobsleds downhill over rock and flower gardens. Even the bunkers to the right are scenic—polka-dotted with grassy mounds.

On the back side, number eleven reaches farther than the members of the Tabernacle Choir set end to end; at 678 yards it's the longest hole in the state. Drive over as much water as you care to consume (carrying 175 to 240 yards in the process), then contend with a bunker pinching the second landing area and two more squeezing in around the huge green. The 467-yard thirteenth is also stellar and psychologically tough. A draw seems like the proper tee shot to avoid bunkers and water right, but such a ball could disappear forever into a ravine on the left. The green here is about as welcoming as a sharp stick in the eye—a hump in the middle of it could kick your approach just about anywhere. Two of Thanksgiving's last four holes are par 3s—of 218 and 250 yards.

Close by Thanksgiving Point, the 7,080-yard **SOUTH MOUNTAIN GOLF CLUB** offers a Vegas-style desert mountain layout brought to you by David Graham and Gary Panks, whose Grayhawk and Raven courses in Arizona are considered among the most sublime dryland venues in the world. Set in the Wasatch Mountain foothills amid wildflowers and chaparral, the vertiginous course offers distant city views.

Elevation changes abound here, as do humps, bumps, and mogully mounds that will carom your shots like an out-of-control downhill skier. The greens tilt every which way. Many of the fairway-side mounds are actually angled to help slightly mishit shots find the short grass, but they also punish severely mishit shots by deflecting them into the pits of hell (okay, actually into ravines and hazards). On many holes, flattish fairways sprout humps closer to the hole, so that longer drives may also have more potential to leave weird side-hill lies. In general, several heavily bunkered holes are often followed by a more simple challenge with no bunkers at all.

Number six is representative of much of the design; this 565-yarder features a wide, flattish landing strip between bunker complexes. If you truly bust a nut off the tee, your ball will careen down among gum-drop mounds, possibly forcing you to lay up on your second shot due to a funky lie. You'll have to hit long and get lucky to have a shot at the green in two, soaring over encroaching dangers en route. Both landing areas here are mined with bunkers: 180 and 238 yards from the tee, then 162 and 227 yards from where your drive will probably alight.

South Mountain's holes carry monikers such as Pioneer Crossing, Red Rock, Courage, and Quick Draw. Number sixteen, Stones, is a short 140 yards but demands a high, soft landing. Even holes that don't kill with length may maim with toughness. The layout ends with a strong 455-yard uphill battle with a stone wall protecting the right side and knocking balls down into a waste area that may require wilderness survival training to escape.

East of downtown, **WASATCH MOUNTAIN STATE PARK** is home to two Bill Neff layouts designed by two different, unrelated Bill Neffs. The older, more traditional **LAKES COURSE** plays to 6,942 yards with eight lakes and little bunkering and has served as a Senior Tour qualifying site. The far more interesting **MOUNTAIN COURSE**, designed by the other Bill Neff, is as purely fun and uncerebral as a roller coaster. The par-71, 6,459-yard layout boasts six par 3s and six par 5s. The front side ends with two 5s, and nearly every hole plays up- or downhill. The greens are flat but canted. Scenery here is the very best of what a perfect autumn day can offer; the surrounding mountains explode with golden yellow aspen and cottonwoods, red maple and oaks, and dependable evergreens.

Wasatch's front side could benefit from a chairlift, as it's nearly all climb starting with the first hole, which doglegs right up a tiered fairway. Number three, a spunky par 3, ascends beside the restored Huber Farmhouse and Creamery, which were built in 1870. Number eight offers a brief respite—a 593-yard downhill hole that is reachable in two. The ninth again requires crampons as it journeys back up for 510 yards. The back nine opens with two short holes of 160 and 290 yards (score well early here)—the latter uphill over a wide, forested gorge. On the 635-yard twelfth, Mark O'Meara once reached the green with driver, six iron. The fourteenth hole, at 366 yards, is narrow enough to use for a luge course.

Just a ski jump from South Mountain lies **THE HOMESTEAD RESORT**, Utah's only full-fledged golf resort. Senior Tour pro Bruce Summerhays—who was the pro at Wasatch Mountain for many years—designed this homey 7,040-yard track. The front nine winds its way up into the mountains, giving up wide views en route. The back nine winds through Snake Creek Valley and assails with water on every hole. If you even whisper the word "putt" (especially on the 184-yard second hole), your ball may scream downhill and roll off the green: I've never seen so many short balls leave the building. Number five presents a very solid 600-yard dogleg right; muscle your drive over the hill at the corner, then avoid the water that begins on the left side 150 yards from the green. A short drive will require cutting blindly over the hill; beware bunkers that narrow in toward the putting surface.

One of the most memorable touches at the Homestead is the double ninth/eighteenth green, which rolls through a grove of cottonwoods, some of which reside in the deep left bunker. The course finishes on the left half of this handsome monster after traversing 448 yards of strategic challenge, including a long carry over a creek.

On your way to returning your cart, why not stop off to swim, snorkel, dive, or soak in the lava dome—a fifty-five-foot open-topped limestone crater filled with hot water? This weird natural phenomenon provides for the only warm water diving within the continental United States. And no, nobody has hit a golf ball into the open crater, as of yet.

If the **BOUNTIFUL RIDGE GOLF COURSE** north of Salt Lake City looks strangely familiar, you've been playing too much video golf. This 6,523-yard Bill Neff design is featured on Access Software's Links golf game. Deftly built into forested foothills, Bountiful's clean, well-crafted holes abound with views of the Great Salt Lake and downtown.

Your trip around Bountiful begins with a 517-yard foray to a green clustered with bunkers. Number eight might be the course's prettiest hole, with streams, waterfalls, and boulders decorating the inside corner of a 310-yard dogleg left. The fifteenth requires a tee shot that skims the top of a scrub oak forest that somehow brings New Hampshire to mind. Oak clumps are a major feature throughout the course, though not to the exclusion of pines, spruce, and other vertical hardwood hazards. Bountiful finishes big with an eighteenth hole that screams, "We had money left over!" The hole cruises for 485 yards; from behind the green emerges a cascade of waterfalls and wildflowers that drop to the base of the hill that holds the putting surface.

The Homestead:
Midway, Utah ▶

Also to the north, in Layton, lies **VALLEY VIEW GOLF COURSE**, designed by William Hull and opened in 1974. Lakes on more than half the holes lend a watery bite to this fine municipal venue that maxes out at 7,147 yards. Not just the valley views are good from the very first hole, a giant slalom of 447 yards that careens downhill toward a lake that can be taken out of play with a fade exactly like mine. The elevated, undulating green features a willow defense system if you're within casting distance of the lake.

Most of the greens at Valley View are sloped back to front, and many holes begin from escalated tees. Number twelve, a 227-yard jaunt to a green encapsulated by bunkers, is just one fine example. The seventeenth hole is also very strong, a par 5 that ascends to a hidden, elevated green hunkered with bunkers in front. You'll want to come in to this one like politician Jim Jeffords, who moved from right to left.

To reach the **WOLF CREEK RESORT** in Eden, you must motor along one of the prettiest canyon drives in America without miscueing into the Ogden River. You'd be wise to invite a local out as your guide for the 6,905-yard golf course trek. Even when he warns you about how the greens will break, though, you won't listen to him because it just doesn't seem possible.

In fact, about five people warned me not to get above the hole on Wolf Creek's greens, and that was before I even teed off. Strangers stopped their cars to shout this at me. It wasn't until I reached the first one that I understood their warnings. And the day's pin positions didn't help much. The pro explained that the superintendent doesn't like to venture too far onto the putting surfaces if he'd been drinking the night before. Wolf Creek is a very good course, but don't expect an easy feel-good round—unless you feel good about three putting (or worse). However, it would be the perfect venue for a little friendly competition.

Of course, Wolf Creek also has tees, bunkers, fairways, and other requisite golf course elements, and they're all good too. The seventh hole combines a number of them beautifully across 429 yards; a waste bunker and creek lie to the left, a line of trees guards the right side, and your second shot must fly a pond but stay short of four pot bunkers loitering behind the green. One charming assistant pro favors the fifteenth hole, which he describes as "long and open, with a devilish green." In fact, I witnessed a certain golf professional (name withheld to protect the guilty—and because he bribed me with a sleeve of Pro V1s) smooth a fifteen-foot chip shot sixty feet past the hole.

157

Just when you think you've figured out these greens, which all slope from back to front, number sixteen doesn't—the perfect ha ha from architect Mark Ballif, who designed this as the Patio Springs Country Club back in 1965.

If you've got a late flight out of Salt Lake City, or a long layover, consider a quick round at **WINGPOINTE GOLF COURSE**, just outside the airport. It's a tribute to architect Arthur Hills that a course in such a lousy location, and with so little service, could still be this good. For one thing, I could've heard the radios in cars speeding past on the adjacent freeway—if not for the loud voices of flight attendants taking drink orders on the planes so close overhead. It was like playing golf through a John Candy movie.

Yet Hills created a subtle masterpiece of 7,101 yards in a swampy, treeless locale. Every hole is meticulously strategy-forged on this course that bills itself as "Utah's Links," in this case the word "links" simply meaning "shaggy." Number three is a good example of thoughtful architecture, allowing you to cut off as much of a lake as you desire. Mounds welcome shots hit to the right of the narrow fairway, and water accompanies you on the left all the way to the green.

Although from a distance the green encourages a run-up shot, a weird crown just in front deflects such shots toward the water or bunkers. The sixth hole features similar protective services.

The seventh hole at Wingpointe is a study in lovely juxtaposition: Four pot bunkers angle from left to right alongside the apron/green, and the narrow lower green tier deflects shots hit short to a back right pin. Number thirteen requires another judgment regarding how far to fade it into the dogleg right. Aim your tee ball at the I-80 sign—there's more room around the blind corner than you think. A grassy swale left of the green balances a bunker floating to the right. Fifteen and sixteen offer solid back-to-back par 5s of 540 and 588 yards, followed by an all-carry par 3 backdropped by the welcoming cityscape of Salt Lake.

If you learn anything from watching the Olympics, it should be to observe the ritual of après-ski, which loosely translated means "several toddies by the fireplace." This tradition can also be adapted to summer golfing, particularly at some of the West's best microbreweries. Try the Emigration Amber at Squatters Brew Pub in Salt Lake or the Polygamy Porter (motto: Why have just one?) at the festive Wasatch Brew Pub in Park City.

BOUNTIFUL RIDGE GOLF COURSE

2430 S Bountiful Boulevard, Bountiful, UT 84010
801-298-6040
Architect/Year: Bill Neff, 1975
Tees/Yardages: 4 sets of tees from 5,098 to 6,523 yards
Season: April to November
Cost: $
Tee times: Up to 6 days in advance for weekdays, up to 5 days in advance for weekends

THE HOMESTEAD RESORT

700 N Homestead Drive, Midway, UT 84049
800-327-7220 • www.homesteadresort.com
Architect/Year: Bruce Summerhays, 1990
Tees/Yardages: 4 sets of tees from 5,091 to 7,040 yards
Season: March to October
Cost: $ to $$
Tee times: Resort guests up to 30 days in advance, nonguests up to 1 week in advance or 30 days in advance with $10 fee

SOUTH MOUNTAIN GOLF CLUB

1247 E Rambling Road, Draper, UT 84020
801-495-0500 • www.parks-recreation.org/gf
Architects/Year: David Graham and Gary Panks, 1998
Tees/Yardages: 5 sets of tees from 5,165 to 7,080 yards
Season: Year-round
Cost: $$
Tee times: Up to 1 week in advance

THANKSGIVING POINT GOLF COURSE

3300 W Clubhouse Drive, Lehi, UT 84043
801-768-7401 • www.thanksgivingpoint.com
Architect/Year: Johnny Miller, 1997
Tees/Yardages: 5 sets of tees from 5,838 to 7,714 yards
Season: March to November
Cost: $$ to $$$$
Tee times: Up to 2 weeks in advance

VALLEY VIEW GOLF COURSE

2501 E Gentile, Layton, UT 84040
801-546-1630
Architect/Year: William Hull, 1975
Tees/Yardages: 4 sets of tees from 5,679 to 7,147 yards
Season: March to October
Cost: $
Tee times: Call Monday for the rest of the week

WASATCH MOUNTAIN STATE PARK

975 W Golf Course Drive, Midway, UT 84049
435-654-0532 • www.uga.org/clubs/wasatch

Lakes Course

Architect/Year: Bill Neff, 1961
Tees/Yardages: 3 sets of tees from 5,573 to 6,942 yards
Season: April to November
Cost: $
Tee times: Up to 1 week in advance

Mountain Course

Architect/Year: Bill Neff Jr., 1998
Tees/Yardages: 3 sets of tees from 5,009 to 6,459 yards
Season: April to November
Cost: $
Tee times: Up to 1 week in advance

WINGPOINTE GOLF COURSE

3602 W 100 N, Salt Lake City, UT 84122
801-575-2345 • www.slcgolf.com
Architect/Year: Arthur Hills, 1991
Tees/Yardages: 4 sets of tees from 5,228 to 7,196 yards
Season: March to November
Cost: $
Tee times: Up to 1 week in advance

WOLF CREEK RESORT

3900 N Wolf Creek Drive, Eden, UT 84310
877-492-1061 • www.wolfcrcckrcsort.com
Architect/Year: Mark Ballif, 1963
Tees/Yardages: 4 sets of tees from 5,345 to 6,784 yards
Season: Memorial Day to Labor Day
Cost: $$ to $$$
Tee times: Up to 1 week in advance

VANCOUVER AND ENVIRONS

VANCOUVER, BRITISH COLUMBIA, is a confident, multicultural metropolis blessed with tangy ethnic restaurants, chic shopping, a startling harbor, and mountain views. While there's plenty to see and do, you could spend your entire visit within the thousand-acre confines of Stanley Park, where locals retreat to bike and hike through old-growth forest, sail, contemplate totem poles, and sip Earl Grey in a cozy teahouse overlooking the water.

If you happen to venture outside the park, the Grouse Mountain aerial tram will lift your spirits, as will treks through Chinatown, Gastown, or along trendy Robson Street. And fans of urban architecture may require neck massages after examining Vancouver's variegated skyline.

◄ *Cordova Bay: Victoria, British Columbia*

Less than an hour from downtown, **WESTWOOD PLATEAU GOLF AND COUNTRY CLUB** gives new meaning to the word "service." At Westwood, it might mean the free continental breakfast for early weekday golfers or the opportunity to have your car detailed while you're out playing the course. Or how about a custom-stocked mini-bar—all evidence that someplace still cares not only about the obvious touches but about creative service, as well.

The 6,770-yard Michael Hurdzan golf course serves up huge views, giant fir trees, ravines, massive granite faces, and greens clinging to precipices. Begin your round with a friendly word about pace; a sign on the first tee reads, "See you in 4:35." Although Westwood opens gently, things toughen up after two short par 4s. The par 3s are all brutal, the third hole being no exception—205 yards of uphill carry over a deep ravine full of stumps and the bodies of weaker golfers. Many of the par 4s here are short but pumped full of trouble around the greens, and holes generally offer few flat lies if you miss the fairways.

The tenth hole contributes long views to Surrey and the Olympic Peninsula, but don't look now: You're facing a tough driving hole with a green that seems to float on the rim of the known world. Number twelve plays 162 yards (all carry) to a stone amphitheater green that you might reach by caroming off the rock face. Or not. The seventeenth points right at Mount Baker, and eighteen streaks along the straightaway of the old auto racetrack the course was built upon.

An hour east of Vancouver lies the **SWAN-E-SET RESORT AND COUNTRY CLUB**, home to a rare nesting pair of Lee Trevino designs that strongly favor a power fade. The property itself, with one private course, strongly favors members over resort guests, but the public course still provides a good walk of 7,000 yards. Though you'll venture out through undeveloped countryside, the massive Scottish-style clubhouse pokes up through the trees every now and again, promising an exceptional lunch. Several water hazards and a small epidemic of faced, sodded bunkers protect the large, fast greens.

Swan-e-set opens with a narrow 535-yard dogleg lined by a dazzling variety of trees. A big hit might reach either water or the house where John Daly stayed in 1995 during the West Coast Classic (the hundreds of Diet Coke cans have since been picked up). Number two offers a risk/reward with two fairways split by bunkers.

The 611-yard tenth is ranked as one of British Columbia's toughest holes. Lakes left and then right and some well-placed trees call for adroit shotmaking—or dumb luck. The fifteenth hole is called Happy's Haven and is a favorite of Shooter McGavin, Happy

Gilmore's rival in the Adam Sandler movie. Keep an eye out for Bob Barker lurking in the bunker looking for a fight. On the eighteenth, kindly avoid hitting into the chef's herb garden; stay left of the big tree in the fairway, dodge the bunkers right, and smooth your approach to a green surrounded by sand.

One of the joys of British Columbian travel is riding the ferries across spectacular inlets ringed by mountains. Vancouver Island lies only a short boat ride across from Vancouver, so climb on board. Once you land in Swartz Bay, head straight south to Victoria, possibly the prettiest city in North America, full of tea shops and alleyways full of flowers and the fragrances of garlic, curry, and fresh-baked goods. The place to stay in Victoria is the hundred-year-old Empress Hotel, which exudes a level of luxury that is positively, well, Victorian. While cruise-ship tourists queue up for the famous afternoon tea service, you could spend about the same money for an unforgettable dinner in the formal dining room. Nearby attractions include whale-watching excursions, tours of Craigdorroch Castle, and the Royal British Columbia Museum. Half an hour north, approximately a gazillion flowers bloom within the Butchart Gardens. As if this weren't enough, the 280-mile-long island is also home to some forty-five golf courses and a man named Arthur Thompson, at 102 the oldest man to ever shoot his age.

Twenty miles from Victoria the Bill Robinson–designed **OLYMPIC VIEW GOLF CLUB** presents a slightly gimmicky routing with perhaps the best scenery ever gathered around the sport. Playing to 6,530 yards, the course encompasses two waterfalls, sixteen lakes, arbutus trees and garry oaks, and mountain, glacier, and water views up the wazoo. I played the course with a single-digit handicap who admitted there wasn't a straight putt of more than ten feet on the whole layout. The holes are brutal around the putting surfaces, with steep pot bunkers and severe, fun-house slopes.

Start thinking early on this short, target venue. The second hole pleads for accuracy off the tee to avoid a rocky slope left. You're okay if you carry 200 yards, but don't slice it or a lake will swallow your ball. At 330 yards, the hole is almost too easy with a good drive. Holes like number eight will lead you to forgive some of the design's

Fairwinds: Nanoose Bay, British Columbia ▶

trickery because of its sheer, feel-good beauty. The four-tiered green beside a waterfall looks like huge corduroy. Number ten might actually elicit weeping as you contemplate the tranquil purity of three pot bunkers cut into the shelf fronting the green, beside a rock wall. The seventeenth is so over the top with beauty it's got enough for an entire course. A huge, Hawaiianesque waterfall behind the green is visible from the tee 417 yards away. The hole plays through a steep, narrow valley past a huge rock column and a Japanese garden reached by crossing a bridge to an island in a still pond.

Also close to Victoria is the stupendous CORDOVA BAY GOLF COURSE, featuring views of Mount Baker, the San Juan Islands, and the Haro Strait. This 6,668-yard Bill Robinson design boasts sublime shot values and neat, classic looks, not to mention 217 varieties of flora. The course is good enough to have hosted two Payless Opens, in 1994 and 1998. Cordova Bay has produced one of the best yardage books of all time, which includes such etiquette tips as "Leave the bunker a better place than you found it," "If we see you plumb bobbing, we will ask you to explain how plumb bobbing actually works," and "If you drag your pull cart over tees and greens, we reserve the right to drive all over your lawn."

Five holes on the front side of this well-marshaled course move

◄ *Westwood Plateau:*
Coquitlam, British Columbia

from right to left. The first dogs in that direction between mounds that reflect distant hills. Deep framing and pot bunkers surround a huge double green that may require dialing an area code for your putt. Number two calls for you to carry your ball over Burnham Creek; as the yardage book says, "If you are faint of heart and your playing partners are not looking, go ahead—carry your ball over Burnham Creek."

The back side at Cordova Bay is noticeably tougher, with more forced carries, trees, and heavily bunkered greens. Number ten plays beside a full 420-yard compliment of water on the left, and requires two forced carries to reach a small two-tiered green also protected by liquid assets. The seventeenth, at 288 yards, is pure challenge, and all carry if you go for it.

North and west of Victoria, much of Vancouver Island is given over to tracts of wilderness filled with bears, remote peaks, and possibly billions of lost golf balls—they have to go somewhere. There are also a few outstanding golf venues, starting with the **FAIRWINDS GOLF AND COUNTRY CLUB** at the Schooner Cove Resort in Nanoose Bay. Overlooking the blue bay and the Georgia Strait, Fairwinds features eleven ponds, water on seventeen holes, more than seventy bunkers, and countless retirees plying the links. The par-71 Les Furber design plays a fey 6,151 from the tips to the oversized greens. Locals here speak with an accent that is enticingly Scottish-sounding.

Fairwinds opens with a tight 310-yarder with a tough green complex. Hit long and right for a clear approach between bunkers that nuzzle this tiered, curvy putting surface. The fourth hole is the number-one handicap, 418 yards long with a creek fronting the severely tiered green and sand wrapped around it. At 296 yards, number nine will tempt you to swing out of your shoes, but two ponds flank the fairway; why not be sensible, hit an iron, and settle for an easy par? Besides, who wants to finish the round without his shoes?

The back nine contains more huge greens, many of which you'll likely reach in regulation, but then you'll face long, swingy putts upon them. Most holes also feature bunker complexes to the left, where they're less likely to be in play. Number ten presents a shortish par 3—easy only if you land on the correct one of three green tiers. Watch for an eagle's nest high in a tree on the thirteenth, and don't forget to admire the huge mountain views looking back from the fifteenth green. Fairwinds finishes nicely with a 518-yarder with lakes right. Position your second shot short of the 150 marker or hone a three-wood between sandwiching fairway bunkers.

Close by to Fairwinds, between Parksville and Qualicum Beach, lies

MORNINGSTAR INTERNATIONAL GOLF COURSE, site of the Canadian Tour's Morningstar Classic from 1994 to 1996. Scott McCarron and Notah Begay both won the Canadian Tour's spring qualifier here before moving on to bigger things. Designed by ubiquitous Alberta native Les Furber, it plays to 7,018 with a whopping slope rating of 144. The links-style track shows off target landing areas, huge rolling greens, fairway moundings, and expansive bunkers and lakes. Great par 3s are only four-eighteenths of the draw here.

The first couple of holes play easily in the open, though mounds rough up the rough on number two, and four bunkers loiter around the tiered green. Number three moves gently into the trees. Furber generally provides good green entrances but not always toward the pin; going for it often requires more risk and skill. The 190-yard eighth is a fine example of that, calling for left-to-right movement to set up a makeable birdie putt.

According to my playing partner, a two-handicap who referred to himself as "the plumber," the twelfth hole has caused more club breaking than any other on Morningstar. He recommended hitting an iron to the "moose pasture," a landing area fronting a marsh. The 404-yard hole exhibits a duet of water and sand by the green. Sixteen claims a beautiful (unless you're in it) pot bunker fronting the green of a 398-yard jaunt requiring a creek crossing on the drive. The eighteenth makes for a long finish: a 474-yarder with a giant waste bunker in front and creek and bunkers right of the tiered green.

Farther up-island, in Courtenay, lies the peppy and gorgeous **CROWN ISLE RESORT AND GOLF COMMUNITY**, whose golf course is only surpassed by some of the best rooms in Canada, replete with fireplaces, Jacuzzi tubs, and starlight ceilings. The clubhouse also elicits superlatives; where else could you smoke a Cuban stogie overlooking a celebrity antique car museum and then emerge beneath a three-story tower of light shining upon a grand spiral staircase? The resort offers golf in concert with diving, kayaking, whale watching, and sailing trips on America's Cup yachts. A deluxe eight-thousand-square-foot spa and sixteen additional villas were recently in the works.

Graham Cook, from Montreal, designed the 7,024-yard links-style golf course with views of the Comox Glacier and the Forbidden Plateau—a name that might apply to some of the greens here. Cook whipped up some tasty bunker placements and delectable shot angles. The course design and service are two steps above that of most other tracks on the island.

On the 359-yard second hole, hit enough to clear the water but not so much to reach four comely bunkers that are angled to welcome

173

fades. Great visuals also characterize the third hole, a 425-yard left dogleg barking for a shot over bunkers but short of water. The layout, which brings architect Bob Cupp to mind, requires thinking about where particular landing sites will move the ball. Number five's scythe blade of a green bent around water is the perfect example; many of the surrounding mounds will kick balls toward the lake.

The back side contains more housing but also such great holes as the double-dogleg fifteenth, a mere 551 yards of puzzlement. The sixteenth is only 183 yards, but they're all good yards, over water, bunkers, and green swales. Beware trees on the seventeenth hole, and be even more afraid of men's night, when you might have to play against pro Jason Andrew, who recently shot a nine-hole 30 using rental clubs and wearing street shoes.

The mid-island locale of Campbell River is most famous for its world-class fishing. Russ Lim, a guide with the rustically cozy Painter's Lodge, can practically catch salmon by holding out a bagel with cream cheese. The lodge makes for a good base camp for a round of golf at nearby **STOREY CREEK GOLF CLUB**. Les Furber carved the track out of dense mixed forest and routed it along a creek that's home to spawning coho, further connecting the sports of fishing and golf. The eminently walkable 6,697-yard course includes five par

3s, five par 5s, and possibly too many doglegs to the left. Holes three through eight play par 3–5–3–5–3–5.

You'll need to learn a draw if the pin is positioned back left on the par-3 third hole at Storey Creek. Number five doglegs widely around bunkers. The holes here are generally friendly and exude a kind of homemade feel. In fact, the club president and other local golfers cleared stumps on many of the fairways. The eleventh hole, which plays 281 yards around a sharp corner guarded by water and a tall pine will have you tempting fate. Many players will go for it only to discover that it requires a perfect rip that carries all the way to the green. Fourteen is also a fine hole, with a lovely green complex waiting at the 367-yard mark and requiring a 185-yard pop to clear water.

The exchange rate for the U.S. dollar throughout Canada provides one more convincing reason to visit our neighbors on a golfing holiday. And if you apply that same exchange rate to your golf score, you should have no trouble shooting in the seventies.

CORDOVA BAY GOLF COURSE

5333 Cordova Bay Road, Victoria, BC Canada V8Y 2L3
866-380-4653 • www.cordovabaygolf.com
Architect/Year: William Robinson, 1991
Tees/Yardages: 4 sets of tees from 5,237 to 6,668 yards
Season: Year-round
Cost: $$
Tee times: No restrictions if booked online

CROWN ISLE RESORT AND GOLF COMMUNITY

399 Clubhouse Drive, Courtenay, BC Canada V9N 9G3
888-338-8439 • www.crownisle.com
Architect/Year: Graham Cooke, 1993
Tees/Yardages: 4 sets of tees from 5,169 to 7,024 yards
Season: Year-round
Cost: $$ to $$$
Tee times: Resort guests up to 1 year in advance,
nonguests up to 30 days in advance

FAIRWINDS GOLF AND COUNTRY CLUB

3730 Fairwinds Drive, Nanoose Bay, BC Canada V9P 9J6
888-781-2777 • www.fairwinds.ca
Architect/Year: Les Furber, 1998
Tees/Yardages: 3 sets of tees from 5,173 to 6,151 yards
Season: Year-round
Cost: $$
Tee times: No restrictions

MORNINGSTAR INTERNATIONAL GOLF COURSE

525 Lowry's Road, Parksville, BC Canada V9P 2R8
800-567-1320 • www.morningstar.bc.ca
Architect/Year: Les Furber, 1990
Tees/Yardages: 4 sets of tees from 5,313 to 7,018 yards
Season: Year-round
Cost: $ to $$
Tee times: Up to 1 year in advance

OLYMPIC VIEW GOLF CLUB

643 Latoria Road, Victoria, BC Canada V9C 3A3
800-446-5322 • www.golfbc.com
Architect/Year: William Robinson, 1990
Tees/Yardages: 4 sets of tees from 5,308 to 6,534 yards
Season: Year-round
Cost: $$ to $$$
Tee times: Up to 1 week in advance

STOREY CREEK GOLF CLUB

300 McGimpsey Road, Campbell River, BC Canada
V9W 6J3
250-923-3673 • www.storeycreek.bc.ca
Architect/Year: Les Furber, 1990
Tees/Yardages: 4 sets of tees from 5,434 to 6,699 yards
Season: Year-round
Cost: $ to $$
Tee times: Up to 1 year in advance within current calendar year

SWAN-E-SET BAY RESORT AND COUNTRY CLUB

16651 Rannie Road, Pitt Meadows, BC Canada B3Y 1Z1
800-235-8188 • www.swaneset.com
Architect/Year: Lee Trevino, 1993
Tees/Yardages: 3 sets of tees from 5,632 to 7,000 yards
Season: Year-round
Cost: $$ to $$$
Tee times: Up to 1 week in advance

WESTWOOD PLATEAU GOLF AND COUNTRY CLUB

3251 Plateau Boulevard, Coquitlam, BC Canada V3E 3B8
800-580-0785 • www.westwoodplateaugolf.bc.ca
Architect/Year: Michael Hurdzan, 1995
Tees/Yardages: 4 sets of tees from 5,514 to 6,770 yards
Season: April to October
Cost: $$$ to $$$$$
Tee times: Up to 1 year in advance

◀ *Swan-e-set: Pitt Meadows, British Columbia*

WHISTLER

LET'S IMAGINE FOR A MOMENT that you've been given the all-encompassing power to create the perfect golf resort destination. Hey, it could happen— just like Phil Mickelson could win a major.

You might very well begin this project by choosing the perfect setting for your resort: perhaps a range of stunning glaciated mountain peaks with a sprinkling of blue lakes nearby, all nestled amid enormous, old-growth forests.

No doubt you'd include world-class hiking and mountain-biking trails, fishing, spas, and bunches of cool places to stay—deluxe condos, sprawling rental houses, a couple of first-rate hotels.

You'd probably also want the resort to encompass a swank European-style village with lots of

◀ *Nicklaus North: Whistler, British Columbia*

designer boutiques, galleries, Cuban cigar stores, eclectic restaurants, and shops selling really cool log furniture.

For golfers, you'd develop a handful of courses—say, four—designed by top architects like Nicklaus, Palmer, Jones, and Cupp.

You might consider laying the whole place down in a country where the people are friendly, welcoming, and speak English with an entertaining lilt, and you'd want it to be the kind of country where you could pay for your breakfast with a U.S. twenty-dollar bill and receive twenty-five dollars back in local currency—which is to say there'd be a favorable exchange rate.

So you can either start from scratch to create such a destination, or simply visit British Columbia's superlative Whistler Resort, which is a midlife crisis waiting to happen. You already hate anyone lucky enough to actually live there. But at least you can come to terms with your anger (after all, you've been given all-encompassing power) and still visit Whistler.

For your first Whistler golf outing, visit the 6,676-yard Arnold Palmer–designed **WHISTLER GOLF CLUB**, which has one lake for every two golf holes and a pair of winding creeks thrown in as a bonus. As Arnie himself has said, "Three things make a great golf course: scenery, challenge, and fun, and my course at Whistler has them all."

Whistler Golf Club: Whistler,
British Columbia ▶

(For the longest time, I thought the three things that make a great golf course were double-wide fairways, free drops, and beer. But anyway. . . .) Whistler Golf Club also provides trees as a major strategic factor, as well as particularly fine short par 4s. The course can actually seem gentle if you play conservatively, but how likely is that?

On the opening hole, you'd be wise to learn from the great Greek philosopher Socrates and avoid the hemlock that's likely to poison your chances for par on this 380-yarder. On number two, a spruce is the troublemaker, loitering 80 yards short and right of the green. The course yardage book offers this warning about the 188-yard eighth hole, named Singing Cedars: "Do not be above the hole. I repeat, do not be above the hole." Aside from the fact that we're worried about Arnie because he's been repeating himself lately, we're planning on staying below the hole— entirely avoiding the weird tier in the center of the green if possible. Seven is one of the best holes on the course—a 356-yard, par-4 romp bisected by a stream. Hit to 140 yards from the green and try rolling one over the bridge and right at the flag, like I did.

The back side opens with Wind Talker, another of the aforementioned fine, short par 4s. This dogleg right skirts a lake left, and Crabapple Creek flows along the right before cutting in front of the green. The 457-yard par-5 sixteenth double dares you to attack the green over water on your second shot. The final hole, Last Run, reinforces the connections between golf and skiing and offers views of Mount Currie and the biggest green of the day.

As in real life, the rivalry between Palmer and Jack Nicklaus extends to our Whistler fantasy—in this case in the form of the competing NICKLAUS NORTH GOLF COURSE. The 6,908-yard track features wide fairways lined with trophy homes and lies on the shores of glacially tinted Green Lake. Do not mistake the lake for an actual green, as it's extremely hard to putt. This par-71 venue has hosted the Skins Game and Shell's Wonderful World of Golf. Jack's design features some especially deep bunkers and routes through wetlands sprouting perky fescues and no shortage of lakes, which are mostly decorative. Only a couple of holes here lack water.

Number four presents the longest four-shot hole at 465 yards. It features one fairway bunker and a green set amid trees and wildflowers. The sixth hole, at 179 yards, shares a double green with number eight. Bunkers surround the putting surface and a left-to-right crosswind will mess with you as you stand on the tee admiring Rainbow Mountain in the distance.

The back nine contains three par 3s that are among the prickliest holes on the course. Ten's 185 yards are protected by water and a trio

of bunkers. You can cheat short and left, but then again you could skip the hole entirely and tell people you shot a lower score. Number twelve, which plays 225 yards to an island green, has been called one of the toughest holes in the province. Its crowned green, which may channel your well-hit shot toward the water, has helped earn it a designation as the number-six handicap hole—unusual for a par 3. In the middle of the back nine the holes turn purer, with fewer hazards, before Green Lake comes into view (and into play) on the fifteenth. Seventeen presents one more long, tough par 3 of 226 yards where a good shot might come in from the left over sand and water to this number-eight handicapper.

Robert Trent Jones Jr. may not give Palmer and Nicklaus much competition in a two-dollar Nassau (although he was a competitive college golfer), but he will give most former touring pros a run for their money both as a poet (he's actually produced a CD of original verse) and as a course designer. Unfortunately, his efforts at the **FAIRMONT CHATEAU WHISTLER GOLF CLUB** may strike you as more of a limerick than a sonnet. Granted, Jones had a very tough piece of mountain property to work with, but some of these holes will just leave you wondering.

The course, built into the side of Blackcomb Mountain, features four hundred feet in elevation changes, which should explain part of

◀ *Fairmont Chateau Whistler,*
British Columbia

the problem. In its favor, though, it makes lovely use of exposed rock faces, ledges, ravines, and waterfalls, not to mention that it offers high views of the Whistler Valley. Also in the plus column, it's associated with the world-class Chateau Whistler hotel.

Many of the greens here slope sharply from back to front, so landing on the correct tier may prove crucial if sometimes unlikely. The first four holes of this mountain mama are a bit—how shall I say—funky? For example, nearly all shots—including putts—on or to the severely canted second green may slide off the putting deck like eggs sliding out of a nonstick pan. Number three is a nearly laughable (that quick, nervous laugh) uphill dogleg left with a blind, hairpin approach over a gaping chasm. At the sixth hole—a plummeting elevator shaft of 163 yards—your ball may hang for half an hour before dropping like a comet to the green. The eighth hole is Chateau Whistler's signature—212 yards to a long, narrow green with water and sand left and a rocky outcropping right. The holes improve markedly on the back side, and by number eleven, which begins the return trip toward the clubhouse, the views may help you forget about the first few holes.

Finish out your quartet of Whistler golf rounds about twenty minutes north of Whistler Village at Bob Cupp's cleanly designed **BIG SKY**

GOLF AND COUNTRY CLUB. The golf holes gather at the base of 8,450-foot Mount Currie, which watches over your round like a sheer, granite deity. Many consider Big Sky the best of the area's golf offerings. The flattish, links-style layout spread out in the Pemberton Valley is perfect for walking. At 1,600 feet lower in elevation than its neighboring courses, conditions here may be the best around early in the season.

Cupp's all-Bentgrass design requires some tactical striking, and most holes carry at least some risk/reward. As at Royal Troon, many of the long holes play into the wind and shorter holes play downwind. Water on twelve holes, generous bailout areas, and greens cuddling up against swales and hollows further characterize the Big Sky experience.

The opening hole defines the purity of the design: It's long (450 yards), straight, and bunkerless. Number two introduces water in the form of a lake that pinches the 413 yards of perfectly coifed fairway. The fourth hole cranks up the drama; water right, then left, then right, then left, then right distracts for 600 yards and makes islands out of each of the landing areas. As the course develops, hazards begin to combine—such as on number seven, a 380-yarder where water bulges into the fairway from the right and three bunkers surround the green.

Number twelve, Great Divide, is also memorable for a creek splitting the fairway into right and left hemispheres. The green lies just to the left of the water. On number eighteen, a stream graduates into a lake on the right, and it cuts into the fairway 40 yards from the green. Sand wraps the right and front of the putting surface.

That's exactly how it might all look if you designed the perfect golf destination. And while you're still wielding all-encompassing power, might you have a moment to do a little something about my slice?

BIG SKY GOLF AND COUNTRY CLUB

1690 Airport Road, Pemberton, BC Canada V0N 2L3
800-668-7900 • www.bigskygolf.com
Architect/Year: Bob Cupp, 1994
Tees/Yardages: 4 sets of tees from 5,208 to 7,001 yards
Season: April to October
Cost: $$ to $$$$$
Tee times: Up to 1 year in advance

FAIRMONT CHATEAU WHISTLER GOLF CLUB

4612 Blackcomb Way, Whistler, BC Canada V0N 1B4
877-938-2092 • www.fairmont.com
Architect/Year: Robert Trent Jones Jr., 1993
Tees/Yardages: 4 sets of tees from 5,157 to 6,635 yards
Season: May to October
Cost: $$$$ to $$$$$
Tee times: No restrictions

NICKLAUS NORTH GOLF COURSE

8080 Nicklaus North Boulevard, Whistler, BC Canada V0N 1B0
800-386-9898 • www.golfbc.com
Architect/Year: Jack Nicklaus, 1995
Tees/Yardages: 5 sets of tees from 4,732 to 6,908 yards
Season: May to October
Cost: $$$$ to $$$$$
Tee times: Up to 6 months in advance

WHISTLER GOLF CLUB

4001 Whistler Way, Whistler, BC Canada V0N 1B4
800-376-1777 • www.whistlergolf.com
Architect/Year: Arnold Palmer, 1983
Tees/Yardages: 3 sets of tees from 5,348 to 6,676 yards
Season: May to October
Cost: $$$ to $$$$$
Tee times: No restrictions

THE OKANAGAN VALLEY

THE RESPONSE OF MY FRIENDS in Portland when I told them I was headed for Kelowna, in the Okanagan Valley, was this:

"Isn't that in Germany?"

They hadn't even heard of this fine Canadian golf and wine-making destination a mere eight-hour drive from our fair city. When I added that I was also headed for Kamloops, they didn't know where that was either, but they seemed to like saying "Kamloops."

The Okanagan Valley lies in fertile high-desert, fruit-growing country between the Cascade and Rocky Mountains. Dusky hills and blue lakes punctuate miles of blossoming orchards and vineyards. In fact, the Okanagan hosts four wine festivals every

◀ *Harvest Golf Club: Kelowna, British Columbia*

year—one each season. It encompasses sixty-five vineyards and stands as the largest producer of ice wine in the world—that sweet, quenching draft made from grapes that have frozen on the vine.

Wineries worth a visit both for sampling a few sips and repasting in their excellent restaurants include Summerhill Estate Winery, which boasts the largest organic vineyards in Canada. A visit to the estate includes free tasting of such lighthearted but sincere wines as their pinot noir ice wine and the slappingly refreshing Ehrnenfelser, as well as a visit to the four-story replica of Egypt's Cheops Pyramid, where the wines are aged. Summerhill's beautifully labeled Enchanted series was good enough to be sipped by the stars at the 2003 pre-Oscar party. And don't miss dinner in the restaurant next to the tasting room, with lovely views out over the vineyards and lake. Just north of town, Gray Monk Cellars also offers the requisite fabulous food, great views, and perky facility tour. Its 2000 chardonnay is a light, grapefruity wine perfect for a summer evening, and its Latitude 50 Gamay and Gray Monk Odyssey Merlot are also worth sneaking back over the border.

In addition to dozens of vineyards, the town of Kelowna sports a charming art district in what was once the center of the local fruit-packing industry. Now six blocks bloom with music, galleries, and

The Quail course at The Okanagan Golf Club: Kelowna, British Columbia ▶

shopping. You might also wander over to the beaches along Lake Okanagan with an eye toward glimpsing Ogopogo, the local monster who lives under the water. Of course, you're more likely to see the giant green sea serpent (there's a two-million-dollar reward for finding him) after a few tastings at local wineries.

You can also take on your own personal monster (such as three-putting or the shanks, et al.) on one of the area's fine and varied golf courses. Fruit and wine aside, the Okanagan is ripe for a golf-focused visit.

Why not stick with our theme and begin at the easygoing **HARVEST GOLF CLUB**, a Graham Cooke design routed through orchards and vineyards that encompass a thousand apple trees of nine varieties, as well as peaches, pears, cherries, and the rare, elusive cobbler and ice-cream trees. The 7,109-yard layout features views of Lake Okanagan from every hole. Cooke cooked up a golden delicious confection of great golf shots defined by easy landing areas from the tees but more demanding approaches to large greens. He made the terrain here even more interesting by developing Bentgrass fairway platforms that seem to float like green islands in seas of thicker blue grass. The edges of the islands fall off toward the club-grabbing rough, creating an aspect of target golf.

The second hole presents a fine example; the 579-yard dogleg left could play a number of different ways, none of them easy. Hit straight at a trio of directional bunkers for the safest play, leaving the longest journey to the green, or take your chances at the corner, where the ocean of rough laps into the fairway. Direct your second shot toward a landing platform that only approaches within a hundred yards of a green surrounded by three pods of three pot bunkers each. The front nine also includes several shots that flirt with water, and a few hit to greens and landing areas not entirely visible from the launch pads. Don't forget to fight cancer by eating some fruit from the encroaching orchards en route (think of it as payback for the trees impinging on some of your shots).

The back side at Harvest opens with unusual Anjou and Bartlett hazards. Number twelve plays underneath a superhighway of bees commuting between blossoms and hives—you'll hear their buzz without seeing the traffic. Both of the par 5s on the return nine play short from the blue tees—479 and 468 yards. Fifteen is the favorite hole of head professional Rob Anderson, perhaps because he won a skin from his assistant there with a birdie the day we played together. The 419-yard challenge turns right around orchards; determining the depth of the green provides part of the challenge. Cap off your round

◀ *Predator Ridge: Vernon,*
British Columbia

here with an outstanding lunch in a restaurant where the entrées do not all feature goofy golf-related names. Or consider coming back to the fine Harvest Dining Room for dinner after changing your spikes and gussying up a bit.

After harvesting a fine round at the Harvest Golf Club, why not step up—literally—to a game at **GALLAGHER'S CANYON GOLF AND COUNTRY CLUB**? The courses here were not named for the bald comedian with the same moniker who invented the Sledge-o-Matic, though you might feel it was after negotiating the 6,802 yards designed by William Robinson and Les Furber.

Gallagher's eighteen-hole routing opens with the number-one handicap hole, 434 downhill yards that might call for a layup unless you catch a mound along the right side of the fairway that will toboggan your tee ball within striking range of the elevated green. Your second shot is better off at the bottom of the hill, in short grass, than with a funky uphill lie in the rough closer in. The sixth hole here was a personal favorite—524 yards with a tough visual of an apparent pit of doom 100 yards out from the green (it's actually an area of unkempt rough growing on a ridge). You'll have to decide between laying up short of the pit or blasting over it. The actual canyon for which the course is named comes into view on the seventh tee, and the ninth tee presents one of the best views of the day: a stream winding through a steep canyon way below. A sign pointing into the canyon reads, "Papa Joe's Green," and local legend suggests it's good luck to smack a ball into the void—though maybe it's most lucky for the kid who retrieves all such shots and sells them back to the pro shop.

Make sure your driver is humming by the ninth hole because three par 5s are coming up in the next four holes, and they all stretch over 500 yards. Yikes! Number thirteen, a 187-yard par 3, features a three-tiered corduroy green that you'd be better off re-teeing to than having to putt on from the wrong tier. Number seventeen plays down in the flats toward some nouveau farm houses; drive over the large poplars guarding the left side of the dogleg left or carry them on the approach, unless your tee shot lasers perfectly to the very right edge of the fairway. On eighteen, avoid a pine tree in your face in the landing area.

Gallagher's also offers the nine-hole **PINNACLE** course. George Orwell might have been inspired by the par-32 layout, which plays to 1,984 yards.

If you liked Gallagher's Canyon, why not give architect Les Furber another chance to deepen your relationship with a little more Furber at **THE OKANAGAN GOLF CLUB** (OCG)? It's located in hilly terrain a runway's length from the Kelowna Airport. Furber's 6,785-yard **QUAIL** course shares 384 acres with the **BEAR** course, executed by Nicklaus Design. The OGC is also home to the John Jacobs Golf School.

You'll need accurate shooting to bring down the Quail, which features dramatic elevation changes, multi-tiered fairways, and the occasional lake and rocky bluff. Although the starter may look at you like you're loony (which, coincidentally, is what Canadians call their dollar—the loonie), the Quail makes for an invigorating walk even if you're not a mountain sheep.

The short opening hole ripples down and to the left for 343 yards. Hit an iron off the tee. Kind moundings may well kick a mishit shot back to fairway. Number two, which hopscotches downhill for 540 yards, offers similarly friendly landings, as well as views of the Rocky Mountains beyond piney hills. Things toughen a bit at number three, with grass craters and a couple of blind shots to a green set in a bowl of mounds. Oh, and there's a tree in the right fairway about 225 yards out.

You could play Okanagan's Quail course every day for the rest of your life and never face the same series of shots. The sixth hole provides just one example—a double dogleg that barks uphill to a blind green after a second blind shot following a drive to one of two fairways separated by a fine sledding hill. Number seven presents one of the layout's many long, tough par 3s that comprise a good chunk of the yardage here. This one tacks on 227 yards, as opposed to the shorter par 3 on the front, which only adds 224 yards.

The back side begins by bringing houses nearly into play (if you play like I do) and offers a brief respite from the best holes. Number twelve growls with a crazy, nasty, skinny, narrow green complex fronted by a ball-swallowing dip. Fourteen offers two flat routes to the green, but nearly all players (unless you snap hook your tee shot) will choose to punch a 190-yard shot to the edge of a lake, leaving wedge into the green. Following the 231-yard par-3 fifteenth, step back into the trees—including one in the middle of the sixteenth fairway. The Quail finishes with a strong burst in the form of a 408-yarder that allows you to blast 240 yards to the edge of a lake that must be carried en route to a toughly entrenched putting dais.

On the OGC's 6,885-yard Bear course, holes thirteen through fifteen are "da bomb," playing in the vicinity of Lake McIver. Do like the television hero of the same name would and manufacture a few brilliant shots using matchsticks and duct tape. Overall, the Bear is more like Pooh or Ben than grizzly: wide and gentle.

Once you've played the top courses around Kelowna, head north forty-five minutes for a visit to what may be one of the finest destination golf resorts you'd expect to find in a place you've never heard of. Outside of Vernon, B.C., **PREDATOR RIDGE GOLF RESORT** combines twenty-seven stellar holes with fifty-eight lovely Craftsman-style villas and cottages. The resort also sports a fine restaurant—all of it in a remote setting that is nearly all about golf (okay, there's a pool, too, and the rest of the stuff is coming soon). The property brings to mind the finer aspects of such other remote resorts as Washington's Desert Canyon and Oregon's Bandon Dunes—two of the most highly regarded destinations in the region. Predator Ridge also features a golf academy that promises you will arrive as prey and leave as predator—and if all goes well, it won't be lost golf balls you're stalking.

The golf here spreads languorously across twelve hundred acres of ponds, streams, pine ridges, dry grasslands, lakes, and wheat grass

The Bear course at The Okanagan Golf Club: Kelowna, British Columbia ▶

meadows. Despite the rugged desert topography, the holes exude a powerful linksy feel. The three nines can combine to play from 5,373 to 7,144 yards. The best eighteen were good enough to garner top ratings among all courses and resorts in Canada and to host both the Xerox BC Open and the 2000 Skins Game, which pitted Fred Couples, Sergio Garcia, Mike Weir, and Phil Mickelson in an event that might be renamed "Who Wants to Be an Even Bigger Millionaire?" Les Furber designed the original holes here, and Trevor Smith—former superintendent—added his own touch with an additional nine. The holes are now seamlessly intermingled.

Although you can see the entire 571 yards of the first hole on the **RED TAIL** nine from the tee, the second shot will play blind and narrow from the first landing area. After a forced layup on your second shot, the green will still lie uphill and out of sight—and in my case, really, really far. I actually used all three of my woods on this hole as I closed in on the target. A maze of mounds, bunkers, and deep grassy swales may cause detours en route. Blind shots abound throughout these golf holes, as at number six, an uphill dogleg right with great mounded bunkers that banana in toward the green.

The **OSPREY** nine, which plays to a par of only 35, opens softly, but every one of the par 4s flaps its wings for more than 400 yards. The sole par 5 covers nearly 600 yards. The two par 3s average 220 yards. Still, this collection is easier and more walkable than the other nines—at least until you reach the misanthropic sixth hole. This 247-yard par 3 falls away to the left at the green. A pin behind the bunker could only have been set by Dr. Evil. At number seven, Osprey assumes character similar to Red Tail by growing tough, hilly, and narrow. The second shot on this 412-yarder drops about 100 million feet and recalls the great eighth hole at Pebble Beach.

If you happen to step into the rest room between the eighteenth and nineteenth holes (you can't quit without playing the third great side), keep an eye out for a poster depicting a hawk attacking a turtle who's wearing a golf cap. The caption reads, "Predator Ridge: Where slow play is not tolerated." I couldn't have put it any better myself.

Now on to the **PEREGRINE** nine, which also features one par 3 and one par 5 and takes us quickly back into the trees. At least the 481-yard par-4 second hole is downhill, even if it leans right, then left, before narrowing between mounds in front of the green. Number five here is named Dangerfield because errant shots get no respect. The green platform sits against a rocky outcropping. Number eight breaks out into the open again with a huge mound farm in the distance. A stone wall supports the left side of a green sitting at the end

of a fairway lined with water. The ninth here is possibly the best finishing hole among the three nines. A stream crossed by a stone bridge and lovely bunkering characterize this 460-yard closer.

Predator Ridge makes the perfect stopover (if staying for a year constitutes a stopover) on the way from Kelowna to Kamloops, where two more layouts await your golf balls. The **SUN RIVERS GOLF RESORT** hangs onto the side of a steep mountain above the North Thompson River. The golf course itself is carved out of benchlands at the base of Mounts Peter and Paul (Mount Mary is nowhere to be seen, and may well be blowin' in the wind that occasionally roars across the golf holes). The elegant residential community built around the course is the only one in Canada heated and cooled with geothermal energy.

Graham Cooke designed the 7,023 yards of golf routed among aromatic sage, small cacti, dryland wildflowers, sand dunes, and sweeping views that, for my money, are far better than views of someone sweeping. Many of the holes unfurl along platforms dug into the mountainside that turn either up or down into the hill—which is a complex way of saying that elevation changes abound.

Experiment on your first drive by hitting into the right sidehill and watching your ball return obediently to the fairway. Good ball! The flat green is tucked back around to the right a mere 580 yards from

◀ *Gallagher's Canyon:*
Kelowna, British Columbia

the tee. One of the elder statesmen—a golf journalist—I played with at Sun Rivers claimed to have hit a 420-yard drive on this hole, thanks to the downhill, downwind booster. Of course, he also thought he was Napoleon. Number three provides an example of a hole that is more visually intimidating than actually difficult. Hit over a pine tree at a directional bunker and try to clear the distant rise. Call the next few holes "patio golf," as they seem to hang out high above the highway, until number six descends nearly all the way to the river. En route, keep an eye out for coyotes and bighorn sheep.

Locals are especially fond of the back nine at Sun Rivers, which ambles away from the highway. Number ten threatens to slide right off the earth. Hit straight down the valley into a *woo-hoo* roller-coaster fairway and avoid the wild grasses lurking to the left on this 630-yard ride. If you can accurately slam a drive 250 yards, you're a better man than I and might have a chance to show off this skill on number eleven, where your drive is everything—or nothing, which is to say you can hit a seven-iron followed by an eight-iron on this sharp, uphill dogleg left if you don't want to tempt fate by swinging for the green. On number fourteen, skootch a five-iron to a cliff edge but beware of overamping and leaving an amusing hanging lie. No worries, though, as the green is a short belay below. The last few holes wander through deep, sagey sandhill canyons. Two of the last four are par 3s, and one other is a 478-yard par 5, so you can give your driver a rest.

If for some reason you find yourself on a lifelong mission to discover the best greens in Canada, look no further than **THE DUNES AT KAMLOOPS**, a 7,131-yard Graham Cooke design carved among sand dunes that were once the bed of the North Thompson River. Bluegrass fairways, Bentgrass greens, fescue, and crested wheat grass spread over dunes as high as twenty-five feet (or about twenty feet given the Canadian exchange rate). The Dunes has won several accolades and hosted the Canadian Tour Qualifying School.

Play with head professional Mike Porco, and you'll wonder two things: why nearly every Canadian foursome includes at least one lefty

Sun Rivers: Kamloops, British Columbia ▶

(theories: from playing hockey or because they want to be Mike Weir) and whether the Canadian PGA executes all golf pros when they turn forty. Porco is one of the new breed of young Canadian pros who can hit the ball and—unlike many of their American counterparts—still have personalities. Play with superintendent Terry Smith here, and you'll worship (or curse) him for the impeccable putting grounds.

The Dunes opens with a 608-yarder framed by pines and chock full of convincing dunes in the swaley, swively fairway. Later, you'll play additional par 5s of 602 and 571 yards. Even from the blue tees, five par

◀ *The Harvest Golf Club:*
Kelowna, British Columbia

4s tough it out over 400 yards. Ouch. Number three provides only one example of Graham Cooke's excellent use of natural waste areas, which are sometimes bigger than the fairways. The sixth hole tunnels between mounds, with more mounds making for difficult lies on the fairway.

Many of the greens here sit upon platforms with bunkers at their bases. Number nine shows off the course's first liquid assets on a dogleg right that turns sharply around a pond wrapped by a curvy bunker that follows the water's contours. You can cut the corner over this mess of potential travesty or take it all out of play by staying far left.

The back side delights even more than the front and looks a bit different as well, as it moves closer to the riparian area beside the river. The tenth green is set at the base of steep, heavily vegetated mounds. Fourteen is the course's signature hole, framed by pines and a deep valley protecting the angled, three-tiered green. The downhill par 3 fifteenth, at 173 yards, is also framed by pines; get too far right and you'll find yourself in a delightful, hilly glade with grassy mini-buttes. The river itself finally comes into view on sixteen. Housing in view from the eighteenth fairway reminds you that your golf journey is over and you're back in civilization—or at least back in housing, if that's any measure of civility compared with the sylvan golf courses of the Okanagan Valley.

THE OKANAGAN VALLEY: *Courses*

THE DUNES AT KAMLOOPS

652 Dunes Drive, Kamloops, BC Canada V2B 8M8
888-881-4653 • www.golfthedunes.com
Architect/Year: Graham Cooke, 1996
Tees/Yardages: 4 sets of tees from 5,441 to 7,131 yards
Season: March to October
Cost: $$
Tee times: No restrictions

GALLAGHER'S CANYON GOLF AND COUNTRY CLUB

4320 Gallagher's Drive W, Kelowna,
BC Canada V1W 3Z9
800-446-5322 • www.golfbc.com
Architects/Years: Bill Robinson, 1979; and Les Furber,
1992
Tees/Yardages: 3 sets of tees from 5,574 to 6,802 yards
Season: April to October
Cost: $$$
Tee times: Up to 30 days in advance

THE HARVEST GOLF CLUB

2725 KLO Road, Kelowna, BC Canada V1W 4S1
800-257-8577 • www.harvestgolf.com
Architect/Year: Graham Cooke, 1994
Tees/Yardages: 4 sets of tees from 5,454 to 7,109 yards
Season: March to October
Cost: $$ to $$$
Tee times: No restrictions

THE OKANAGAN GOLF CLUB

3200 Via Centrale, Kelowna, BC Canada V1V 2A4
800-446-5322 • www.golfbc.com

The Quail

Architect/Year: Les Furber, 1992
Tees/Yardages: 5 sets of tees from 4,713 to 6,785 yards
Season: April to October
Cost: $$$
Tee times: Up to 30 days in advance

The Bear

Architect/Year: Nicklaus Design, 1999
Tees/Yardages: 5 sets of tees from 5,100 to 6,885 yards
Season: April to October
Cost: $$$
Tee times: Up to 30 days in advance

PREDATOR RIDGE GOLF RESORT

301 Village Centre Place, Vernon, BC Canada V1H 1T2
888-578-6688 • www.predatorridge.com

Red Tail (nine holes)

Architect/Year: Les Furber, 1991
Tees/Yardages: 4 sets of tees from 2,686-3,578 yards
Season: April to October
Cost: $$$
Tee times: Up to 1 year in advance

Osprey Course (nine holes)

Architect/Year: Les Furber, 1991
Tees/Yardages: 4 sets of tees from 2,687- 3,521 yards
Season: April to October
Cost: $$$
Tee times: Up to 1 year in advance

Peregrine Course (nine holes)

Architect/Year: Les Furber, 1991
Tees/Yardages: 2,827-3,566 yards
Season: April to October
Cost: $$$
Tee times: Up to 1 year in advance

SUN RIVERS GOLF RESORT

300 Mariposa Court, Kamloops, BC Canada V2H 1R3
866-571-7888 • www.sunrivers.com
Architect/Year: Graham Cooke, 2001
Tees/Yardages: 4 sets of tees from 4,940 to 7,023 yards
Season: March to October
Cost: $$
Tee times: No restrictions

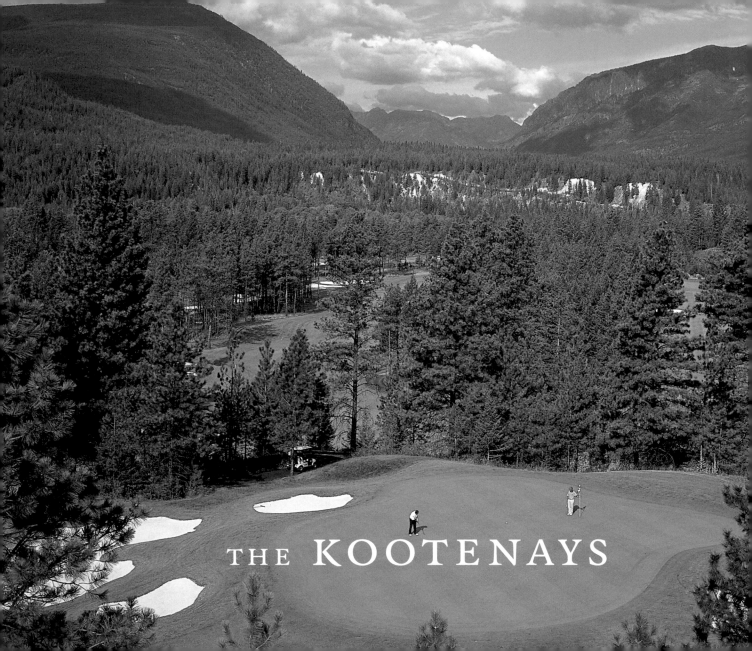

THE KOOTENAYS

IT'S TOUGH having famous neighbors. For Canada's Kootenays region, forced anonymity from its proximity to such other great northern golf destinations as Whistler, Vancouver, Banff, and the Okanagan has left the courses here on the western edge of the Rocky Mountain chain well priced and not overly crowded. Lonely, even. Yet the Kootenays still proffer equally stunning mountain views, outdoor adventures aplenty, and some wild Old West history in a friendly and peaceful destination. Not to mention the always-popular Canadian exchange rate. Why not cheer the Kootenays up by paying a visit?

While you're there, you can play as many as seven fine golf layouts luxuriating across valleys, beside roaring rivers, carved into mountains, and routing

◀ *Bootleg Gap: Kimberley, British Columbia*

213

along steep bluffs that appear to float between mountains and valleys. If you're a bit breathless during your visit, it may be more than the scenery: These courses nestle at as high as 4,000 feet of altitude, making for a slightly tougher walk but also longer drives.

Start your Kootenays golf adventure at the **ST. EUGENE MISSION GOLF RESORT**, close by the Cranbrook Airport. Your own mission at St. Eugene involves taking on a links-style venue that plays through flatlands beside the St. Mary River and generously doles out views of high, distant peaks. Occasional forays into pine forests help to establish a nice rhythm of holes. This classic Les Furber design stretches to 7,007 yards, with an emphasis on rewarding good shots. Those hit accurately toward target bunkers and 150-yard poles will set up the best approaches into the large, deep greens. Golf purists will enjoy the clean look and clear options presented by these holes. St. Eugene also makes for a great nature walk as no housing intrudes upon the golf.

The opening holes are simply darned good all the way to number seven, an even more outstanding 212-yard downhill par 3 with a green that falls away in the back like a drunk toward a deep collection bowl. The ninth hole, a par 5 stretching to as long as 556 yards, calls for a draw hit over the fast-moving river at a pair of directional bunkers, followed shortly by an approach lasered between riverside moundings and a pond. The back side opens with a 569-yard par 5 that plays to a double green. This nine consists of three par 3s, three par 4s, and three par 5s and finishes 3–5–3–5. On the final hole, bust a drive over a mid-fairway bunker to earn a chance at carrying wide Joseph's Creek on your second shot to a green set in the shadow of the 1912 former mission building currently housing resort guest rooms.

Twenty minutes north of Cranbrook lies **BOOTLEG GAP GOLF**, which has cryptically dropped the word "Course" from the end of its name. The newest among Kootenay Rockies golf venues, this young muni upstart designed by the ubiquitous Les Furber stretches to 7,157 yards along bluffs and hoodoos high above the St. Mary River. Although Bootleg could still benefit from further grow-in time, it promises to deliver a fine lower-priced alternative to other area

St. Eugene Mission: Cranbrook, British Columbia ▶

215

tracks. Featuring some very difficult shots to front or back pins set on sloping greens, the course forces you to work with the terrain to shoot a low score. A number of holes play right at Bootleg Mountain and the gap between it and neighboring peaks.

Number five, at 520 yards, demands a very tough, narrow approach that must avoid a canyon that you can't see lurking in front of a bunker 150 yards from the green. The par-3 twelfth, with a seventy-foot drop, begins a three-hole stretch along the river. Thirteen, a slight dogleg right over another ravine, drops sharply; the river runs in the distance far left and a big pine near the tee box narrows the

◀ Trickle Creek: Kimberley, British Columbia

216

available real estate for faders. My droll British playing partner, upon observing my prodigious slice here, remarked that the ninety-degree rule was meant to apply to carts, not tee shots. Bootleg also offers play on a perky par-34 nine-hole layout that tips out at 2,675 yards.

Forty-five minutes north of Cranbrook, the four-season resort area around the Bavarian-themed town of Kimberley is perfectly situated to serve as a home base for playing another handful of the Kootenays best golf venues. Plus, you can order an excellent schnitzel at the Bauerenhaus Restaurant, a 350-year-old structure that was relocated here from Munich. And no, that's not a weird dream: If you're visiting during July, you might catch a few notes drifting over from the Old Time Accordion Championships. So hoist a stein of Kokanee Beer and shout "Wunderbar!" at the top of your lungs.

Begin golfing on your northward journey with a stop at the **EAGLE RANCH GOLF RESORT** in Invermere, where architect Bill Robinson's design encompasses rolling canyons and high hillside bluffs overlooking the Columbia River. Although Heracleitus claimed that you can't swim in the same river twice, this is the same Columbia you may have hit golf balls nearly into at Skamania Lodge and Desert Canyon in Washington state. The 6,637-yard track proffers views of the Columbia Valley, Lake Windermere, and the Rocky and Purcell

Mountains. The front side provides a good first act, with a number of well-manicured but only moderately inspired holes. Take number one for example—this blind 491-yard romp features a maze of mounds and swales in front of the green and a gaggle of trees to avoid en route. It's followed by a series of perfectly polite but unexciting holes. The drama builds on the back side, however, where ravine carries ratchet up the tingle factor on four separate occasions. The 173-yard sixteenth hole plays to a sandstone-guarded green eighty feet below the tee.

Just outside of Kimberley lies the **TRICKLE CREEK GOLF RESORT**, associated with a fine slopeside Marriott Residence Inn featuring stone pillars and wood beams. This 6,896-yard Les Furber design schussing across the slopes of North Star Mountain is like an invigorating ski run in steep moguls: Stay alert and prepare for a rollicking ride with a few startling bumps along the way. Long hitters may be disappointed not to have more opportunities to swing the big stick, as accuracy is at a premium here, especially off the tee. In fact, you won't even pull out your driver until the fourth hole, a 530-yard romp with an all-carry approach shot over a creek that runs down the right side and veers across in front of the green.

The back side opens with an entertaining 333-yarder requiring a tee shot drop zoned onto a platform wedged between a ravine carry and a long dip to the green. Number eleven is the signature hole here—174 downhill yards with epic views from the elevated tee. Trickle Creek may elicit an occasional eye roll, but like a good date it always remains fun.

A side trip to the resort area of Panorama (and its fine village accommodations) should elicit a few howls because it's home to **GREYWOLF GOLF COURSE AT PANORAMA VILLAGE**, clearly the leader of the pack of Kootenays tracks. Greywolf's 7,140-yard Doug Carrick design combines the best of mountain golf with subtle strategic elements that allow you to play some holes in a half-dozen different ways (although not all on the same day). Fairways plummet along fall lines, and greens hug cliff tops on the edges of unbroken forestland. Clear, bubbling creeks provide a calming soundtrack of white noise. The strong par 5s here, in particular, are among the most cerebral fun you'll have anywhere—like a good mystery. Carrick, a student of the work of Stanley Thompson, makes ample use of both directional and carry bunkers.

The opening stretch of holes lopes happily and gently uphill before prancing steeply back down. The farther you hit your drive (and based on whether you have a flat lie) on number three, a

513-yard enigma, the tougher your decision: Carry pods of bunkers with an assault on the green or lay up in one of several different places. The sixth hole, Cliffhanger, only calls for one decision: what club to hit to the green around which the rest of the course was built. You'll bark at the moon as your 200-yard tee shot ascends above Hopeful Canyon and—hopefully—lands on a putting platform balanced atop vertical cliffs. There's not a human-made structure in sight—only steep slopes crowded with galleries full of aspen, fir, and pine.

Number eleven presents a 339-yard temptress with a stripe of fairway laid between a lake and a steep hill. Some may consider going for the green off the tee, but then some may lose five balls trying. Fourteen is a 527-yard puzzler with nearly as many optional ways of playing it. With Bentgrass carpeting unfurling from tees to greens, Greywolf may appear soft and furry at times, but it's capable of delivering a sharp bite.

Even farther north and well on your way toward Banff—which will have to wait for another guidebook—lies the **RADIUM HOT SPRINGS RESORT**. As you gaze even *farther* north—toward the Arctic Circle—you may notice a little something called the Rocky Mountains to your right, as well as the Purcell Range to your left. Radium's Les Furber–designed **SPRINGS COURSE** plays to 6,767 yards from the scary black tees and offers one delight after another. The classic styling of the holes brings to mind a giant green Cadillac with big-old fins. The course sits on bluffs high above the Columbia River; looking down, it's easy to imagine that a herd of buffalo just galloped out of view.

The second hole on the Springs Course should wake anyone from a sound sleep: This 396-yard dogleg left boasts a humongous wooden sandbox on the edge of a canyon at the corner and a second shot played straight up into the stratosphere over dauntingly deep lines of bunkering. Number four, at 185 yards, features a wooden-faced bunker in front of and a pot bunker behind the green. Seventeen provides another memorable par-3 experience—149 yards to a large but very shallow green. Don't go looking for your ball if you miss short as it will have tumbled some thirteen thousand miles to the bottom of a ravine. Radium also offers play on the yardage-challenged (i.e., short) RESORT COURSE, coincidentally located just down the road from the Springs Course at the welcoming resort.

Just in case you feel you haven't covered enough territory in the Kootenays, there's one more course worth visiting that couldn't be more out of the way, which may be its greatest charm. If you're headed back the two hours to Cranbrook, why not venture an additional two-and-a-half hours down to Creston and then back up along

Kootenay Lake to the pleasingly remote **KOKANEE SPRINGS GOLF RESORT**. Even the journey to Crawford Bay at the very end of the lake should bring to mind out-of-the-way New England destinations. Except of course for the giant mountains in the distance, and the glacier, and the humongous trees. But the remote quaintness is similar. At least a little. I think.

At any rate, the Norman Woods–designed golf course (Woods was an apprentice of Stanley Thompson and designed several hundred courses of his own) exudes a nostalgic, old-timey feel as it plunges and climbs through thick forests and eventually climaxes in the flats of a beautiful valley where they've taken grass growing to a new level. The opening holes here play breezily downward—all the way to number five, a 462-yard sled hill that poses a second-shot choice between laying up short of or carrying a rollicking creek fronting the deep, narrow green. Although nearly every hole here is well-designed and entertaining, the highlight comes on the last stretch, where lakes and rock walls and greens set into forest alcoves might elicit a few appreciative sighs. The seventeenth, a tight 556 yards with a green guarded by apple trees, may require two or three draws. Following golf, enjoy a tasty clubhouse meal and then stay at the resort so you can dash back out for your early tee time tomorrow.

BOOTLEG GAP GOLF

400 315th Avenue, Kimberley, BC Canada V1A 3G9
877-427-7077 • www.bootleggapgolf.com
Architect/Year: Les Furber, 2002
Tees/Yardages: 4 sets of tees from 5,465 to 7,157 yards
Season: April to October
Cost: $$
Tee times: No restrictions

EAGLE RANCH GOLF RESORT

RR #3 M-2 C-11, Invermere, BC Canada V0A 1K3
877-877-3889 • www.eagleranchresort.com
Architect/Year: William Robinson, 2000
Tees/Yardages: 4 sets of tees from 5,086 to 6,637 yards
Season: April to October
Cost: $$ to $$$
Tee times: No restrictions

GREYWOLF GOLF COURSE AT PANORAMA VILLAGE

1660 Greywolf Drive, Panorama, BC Canada V0A 1T0
800-663-2929 • www.greywolfgolf.com
Architect/Year: Doug Carrick, 1999
Tees/Yardages: 4 sets of tees from 5,400 to 7,140 yards
Season: May to October
Cost: $$$ to $$$$
Tee times: No restrictions

KOKANEE SPRINGS GOLF RESORT

16082 Woolgar Road, Crawford Bay, BC Canada V0B 1E0
250-227-9226 • www.kokaneesprings.com
Architect/Year: Norman Woods, 1968
Tees/Yardages: 3 sets of tees from 5,747 to 6,604 yards
Season: April to October
Cost: $$
Tee times: No restrictions

RADIUM HOT SPRINGS RESORT

8100 Golf Course Road, Radium Hot Springs, BC
Canada V0A 1M0
800-667-6444 • www.radiumresort.com

Springs Course

Architect/Year: Les Furber, 1988
Tees/Yardages: 4 sets of tees from 5,163 to 6,767 yards
Season: March to October
Cost: $$ to $$$
Tee times: Up to 8 months in advance

Resort Course

Architect/Year: Graham Cooke (renovation 1996), 1957
Tees/Yardages: 2 sets of tees from 4,752 to 5,475 yards
Season: March to October
Cost: $ to $$
Tee times: Up to 8 months in advance

ST. EUGENE MISSION GOLF RESORT

7731 Mission Road, Cranbrook, BC Canada V1C 7E5
877-417-3133 • www.golfsteugene.com
Architect/Year: Les Furber, 2000
Tees/Yardages: 4 sets of tees from 5,388 to 7,007 yards
Season: April to October
Cost: $$ to $$$
Tee times: No restrictions

TRICKLE CREEK GOLF RESORT

500 Gerry Sorenson Way, Kimberley, BC Canada V1A 2Y6
888-874-2553 • www.tricklecreek.com
Architect/Year: Les Furber, 1992
Tees/Yardages: 4 sets of tees from 5,725 to 6,896 yards
Season: May to October
Cost: $$ to $$$
Tee times: Up to 1 year in advance

Photo Credits

PAGE IX: Courtesy of Swan-e-set
Bay Resort and Country Club

PAGE XII: ©John and Jeannine
Henebry

PAGE 4: ©Rick Shafer

PAGE 9: ©Rick Shafer

PAGE 12: Courtesy of Sandpines
Golf Links

PAGE 16: ©Robert Graves

PAGE 19: ©Rick Shafer

PAGE 22: ©Rob Perry

PAGE 27: ©Rick Shafer

PAGE 28: ©Rick Shafer

PAGE 33: Courtesy of Resort at
the Mountain

PAGE 38: ©Mike Houska/DogLeg
Studios

PAGE 43: ©Rick Shafer

PAGE 46: ©Rick Shafer

PAGE 49: ©John R. Johnson

PAGE 50: ©Mike Houska/DogLeg
Studios

PAGE 52: ©Rick Shafer

PAGE 60: ©Rob Perry

PAGE 65: Courtesy of Eagle Point
Golf Course

PAGE 66: ©Rob Perry

PAGE 69: ©Rob Perry

PAGE 72: ©Rob Perry

PAGE 75: ©Rob Perry

PAGE 78: ©Rob Perry

PAGE 81: Courtesy of Port Ludlow
Golf Course

PAGE 88: ©Rob Perry

PAGE 93: Courtesy of Homestead
Farms Golf Resort

PAGE 98: ©John R. Johnson

PAGE 105: Courtesy of Dolce
Skamania Lodge

PAGE 106: ©Rob Perry

PAGE 111: ©Rob Perry

PAGE 114: ©Rob Perry

PAGE 126: ©John and Jeannine
Henebry

PAGE 131: Courtesy of Whitetail
Club

PAGE 132: ©Klemme/Golfoto

PAGE 135: ©Klemme/Golfoto

PAGE 136: ©Klemme/Golfoto

PAGE 139: ©Klemme/Golfoto

PAGE 140: ©Klemme/Golfoto

PAGE 146: Courtesy of Bountiful
Ridge Golf Course

PAGE 148: Courtesy of
Thanksgiving Point
Golf Course

PAGE 155: ©John R. Johnson

PAGE 162: Courtesy of Cordova
Bay Golf Course

PAGE 167: Courtesy of Fairwinds
Golf and Country Club

PAGE 168: Courtesy of
Westwood Plateau Golf and
Country Club

PAGE 176: Courtesy of Swan-e-set
Bay Resort and Country Club

PAGE 178: ©John and Jeannine
Henebry

PAGE 181: ©Whistler Resort
Association

PAGE 184: Courtesy of Fairmont
Chateau Whister

PAGE 190: ©John and Jeannine
Henebry

PAGE 193: Courtesy of the
Okanagan Golf Club

PAGE 196: ©Gordon Wylie

PAGE 201: ©Gordon Wylie

PAGE 204: ©John and Jeannine
Henebry

PAGE 207: ©Don Weixl

PAGE 208: Courtesy of The Harvest
Golf Club

PAGE 212: ©Don Weixl

PAGE 215: ©Don Weixl

PAGE 216: ©Cran Photo

Index

About the Author

JEFF WALLACH is the author of four previous books: *Beyond The Fairway: Zen Lessons, Insights, and Inner Attitudes of Golf; What The River Says: Whitewater Journeys Along the Inner Frontier; Breaking 100: Eugene Country Club's First Century;* and *Driven To Extremes: Uncommon Tales from Golf's Unmanicured Terrain.*

Wallach has also written more than 500 features, columns, essays, and reviews for such publications as *Outside, Men's Journal, Sports Illustrated, GOLF Magazine, Travel & Leisure Golf, Men's Health,* and *Money.* Wallach is also a founder of The Critical Faculty, a consulting, secret shopping, and media/marketing firm specializing in golf and travel.

Wallach holds a bachelor's degree in English from Vassar College, and a master's in writing from Brown University. He lives in Portland, Oregon.